Your Ever Growing Income:

The Rising Yield on Investments

Henry Mah, CMA

Disclaimer

The information and opinions in this book must not be considered investment advice. The information is intended to be for informational purposes only. I am not an investment advisor and I am not recommending any security or investment product.

Opinions offered here can never be a substitution for independent analysis and due diligence. The book may contain some forward-looking statements and opinions on subject matter that is familiar and already well-covered. Your guess as to the future value of any security is as good as mine, or that of a broker. Forecasting is an unreliable enterprise.

There are always risks involved with investing and investors must expect occasional losses on the risk they take. It is certain there will be periods of time when all investing strategies, including dividend growth investing, will underperform the market. It is always best to have measured expectations when approaching investing in any form.

I dedicate this book to my lifelong partner, Raelene, my son Troy, daughter Theresa, her husband Alain, our grandkids Gabby and Sam and my sister Alice.

To Tom Connolly, I'm grateful for allowing me to borrow so many of his thoughts and ideas for this book.

Special thanks to Theresa, Alain and Sam for their help with editing and the cover artwork.

Amendment

As of December 31, 2020, ShareOwners Investment Inc. will merge with its other half WealthSimple and will no longer exist as a separate investment broker.

Rather than edit this book, eliminating all reference to ShareOwners and fractional shares, I've decided to leave the explanations and examples of full dividend reinvestment, if for no other reason than to show how beneficial it is to be able to buy fractions of shares with new stock purchases and dividend reinvestments.

The only investment vehicle where one will be able to utilize Fill Dividend Reinvestment, and the purchasing of fractions of shares, is by opening a company dividend reinvestment plan (DRIP) account, which is discussed in this book and more fully in "Your Ever Growing Income".

Table of Contents

Foreword

When Henry asked me to prepare a few words by way of a foreword for his great new book, I was in the middle of tallying up our 2018 dividends. It is something we do every November: detail our yearly dividend increases. It does not take long: I hold five stocks, my wife six and the dividend changes have already been recorded by hand as they occur during the year on a wee chart up on the tack board in the laundry room. (There are columns for: buy date, number of shares and price; original yield and dividend; and yield on cost. We change the dividend and yield on cost when it occurs.) Each time my wife's dividends increase, I get taken out to lunch.

This year, though, we are most excited. One of our stocks, Bank of Nova Scotia (BNS), is approaching 100%. One hundred percent of what? When we purchased our BNS in 1990, the dividend was 25¢ a share. Now they send us $3.40 dividend per share every year. Now for the magic of dividend growth; Henry's book will explain it for you in very simple terms. You've heard of stock splits, perhaps. Splits occur every 10 to 15 years on quality growth stocks. Anyway, since 1990 our BNS has had two, 2:1 splits. So, our original price of $14.56, when divided by 4 begets $3.64. On the other side of the coin, our original 200 shares became 400 shares on the first 2:1 split and 800 shares on the second 2:1 split. Look at things this way. We paid $3.64 for our shares and these shares now pay us $3.40 in dividends. We are just about receiving the full amount we paid for the shares back each year (it is actually 93.4%) by way of dividends. Most folks do not know that quality stocks become safer as companies build wealth. AND, and, this is a very important 'and', our 200 shares are now 800 shares (with the splits) and the current price is somewhere close to $70 per share. Does this seem a bit complicated? It's not. It's wonderful! Our income from BNS has grown (to $2,720 a year) and our capital has grown (to $56,000). It is growth that builds these returns; good companies grow: They grow their earnings, they deploy retained earnings properly and they grow their dividends. Learn how this all works from Henry's book and share in the wealth. Henry is convincing; he knows his material well and he employs good examples.

As you are most likely just beginning with dividend growth, some of what you encounter may have to be taken on faith for a while. It is truly unbelievable. This happened to me when I first encountered dividend growth in a 1984, Letter to the Editor of the *Financial Times*. Over the years though, our faith has been confirmed with real cash flow. Hold for it!

*Here is how the BNS steadily grew over the years from 1990: .25, .25, .26, .28, .29, .31, .33, .36, .55, .66, .76 in 2000, .87, .96, .98, $1.10, 1.32, 1.50, 1.74, 1.92, 1.96, 1.96 again in 2010, $2.05, 2.19, 2.39, 2.56, 2.72, 2.88, 3.05, 3.28, and now in 2018, .85 quarterly x 4 = $3.40 a year. We are living the dream . . . building wealth through dividend increases, which, in concert with well deployed retained earnings, drive capital gains in a commensurate amount. I've never, ever, seen a fund increase their distributions like this. Build your own portfolio, with Henry's help.

TOM CONNOLLY
Publisher of: *The Connolly Report* since 1981
www.dividendgrowth.ca

Preface:

Before we get started, I'd like to highlight a few items that you should keep in mind when reading through my book:

1. I am not an academic and, therefore, there will be no past analytical data, forecasting or comparisons to other strategies.
2. I do not present any charts on how well one might do with this strategy or assumptions on potential earnings.
3. I don't provide sample portfolios or a list of recommended stocks.
4. Every effort will be made to provide you with clear and precise steps on the strategy I propose.
5. Examples provided are from accounts I am familiar with and represent real numbers.
6. Examples presented are not a guarantee of similar success in the future, but as real-world results of practicing the process I recommend.
7. There will be no reference to current market value throughout the book, such as: "This portfolio is now worth... $" or "We have beat the market by...% over the past...years".
8. This book will present and explain a process for you to follow. Much of the information will detail a step-by-step process much like a workbook or exercise book.
9. I will try to avoid recommending individual stocks, instead I'll provide you with the task of evaluating stocks on your own with a set of guidelines, showing you how to gather the data, how to analyze the data (as best I can) and allow you to decide whether a stock qualifies.

10. Once you have established your own list of stocks by following my process, you will only repeat the process if you wish and apply it to different stocks or indexes.
11. This book was written specifically for the Canadian investor, but the strategy I propose will work as well in any country. You will select from your particular index or stocks and apply the steps outlined in the book in the manner described. You may also need to find an online source should the sites we use not provide the data on your indexes or stocks.
12. The process will not become outdated over time. The status of the companies may change, but the process will continue to screen out those which do not meet your requirements.

Now, onwards and upwards, as they say!

The No Win Scenario: The Market Kobayashi Maru!

If you're a science fiction buff like I am, you will be familiar with the Kobayashi Maru scenario from Star Trek. In its construction, the Kobayashi Maru is a no-win scenario. James T. Kirk was the only one to ever beat the Kobayashi Maru — by reprogramming the simulation so that it was possible to win. Clever filmmaking, but also a very clever lesson used by many to illustrate a very important point. The only way to win a no-win scenario is to change the rules, or simply don't play their game.

I believe to a certain extent that trying to beat the market, relying on market timing and depending on market returns is a bit like a no-win scenario, or trying to beat the house in a casino. You win via luck; you lose by design.

I am offering you a solution to the Market Kobayashi Maru with:

- A philosophy that beats the "sleight of hand" of market timing.
- A system that eliminates the "best guess" way of stock picking.
- An evaluation system which is simple, effective and allows you to quickly identify quality stocks.
- An alternative to seeking market returns and eliminating the reliance on market returns.
- A system where your returns are not tied to price fluctuations and won't play a part in your investment decisions.

Don't play their game, play yours.

With this book, we are not going to play the price game. Certainly, the goal is to purchase stocks, keeping in mind there are no guarantees in investing, just as there are no guarantees in life. But we'll change the game so that it works to your benefit by providing you with results that are measured, not by price or the direction of the market, but with you having greater control over your returns, where you will be able to see those returns grow.

We're not going to play their game of needing to beat the market, rather, we'll play our own game, with our own rules, ignoring the market altogether!

Introduction:

Income growth is not a difficult concept to grasp, and there is no doubt that it is important, but the topic is rarely mentioned-- even in prominent publications. (Tom Connolly, *The Connolly Report*, Dec. 1994)

Why should you listen to me or take my advice? You shouldn't!

What I hope you will do is take the time to read the book in its entirety, it's not long, and decide if it might be a strategy suitable for you. I don't want you to take anyone's suggestions or advice point blank. You need to determine your personal investing goals. Nothing replaces due diligence and research, even with the strategy that I propose.

> *"73.6% of all statistics are made up"*-Business Insider

> *"85% of statistics are false or misleading"*- World Science Festival

I think it's important to stress the trouble with statistics. There is always "more than one way to skin a cat", as they say, just as there are many ways to achieve one's goal from investing. Some investors like the excitement of daily trading, others do extensive research, charting and forecasting, some believe in Passive Exchange Traded Funds (ETF), and there are those who feel owning everything in every market produces superior results. Don't rely too heavily on others' achievements, tips, stats, "inside information". I have always found the only truth is that some strategies are easy, others complex, some work some of the time, but none work all of the time.

Whether you are a new or a seasoned investor, you may find investing overwhelming. What to buy, when, how much, which markets, who to listen to and finally, when you do buy, and have you made a good choice?

I'll address these questions and suggest an investing strategy from a different viewpoint than most:

- Instead of concentrating on capital appreciation (price of your stocks rising), we will focus on the income your stocks generate.
- Instead of comparing your returns to market indexes or other common benchmarks, we will measure your income growth.
- Instead of worrying about being fully diversified (spreading your investments "across the board"), we will concentrate on selecting a few of the best stocks.
- Instead of providing you with a list of recommended stocks or sample portfolios, **you** will learn to evaluate the stocks and decide which best suits your needs.

In this book I will be demonstrating a method of finding stocks, stock evaluation, and then suggest the best way to make these stocks generate the most income.

- You won't be constantly looking for new stocks to buy.
- You won't need to jump on the latest "hot" stock (like Netflix or the "cannabis craze").
- You won't be monitoring the price of your stocks, worrying when the market changes direction or be concerned should the value of your portfolio drop.
- You won't have to wait until the end of the year to see how your investment strategy is working. You will receive confirmation updates each month or quarter.
- You will, over time, learn to ignore stock prices and market fluctuations.

What exactly am I proposing? Well, quite simply, the following quote from *The Connolly Report,* (a bi-monthly publication on dividend growth investing, published since 1981) describes it best:

"If a company does not pay a dividend, don't buy it. If it doesn't grow the dividend don't buy it either."

That's basically it! It didn't strike home with me immediately, but every time I thought about investing in a particular stock, I kept going back to that simple statement and asking the question, does it pay a dividend and has the dividend grown?

The more I looked into dividends and dividend growth investing, the more sense it made. As I began to understand the strategy and the unique method of stock evaluation, the more convinced I became that dividend growth investing was the way to go.

The Connolly Report evaluates stocks by yield, Graham Value, cyclically adjusted price-to-earnings ratio, and compound annual growth rate. Tom Connolly presents a list of stocks which meet his criteria for the benefit of his subscribers, so they can determine which stocks are expensive (to buy) and compare the different evaluation methods to assist in determining value (a reasonable price to buy). These are great tools and information and have gained Tom a lot of followers and admirers.

I will present a slightly different approach than Connolly's, one where you will evaluate and select which stocks to add to your own portfolio. It's not a fill-in-the-blank, or do-what-I-say strategy, but one where we will provide you with a process to follow but you will do the footwork and come to your own conclusions. You won't need to study company financial statements, project future earnings or perform any other complicated and extensive analysis. I'll present you with a simple, straight-forward and easy method of evaluating and screening out stocks. Our goal is not to find the most stocks, but a select few which will help you achieve a clear and obtainable objective: to provide you with a **growing income from your investments.**

One final note, most of the financial examples used in the book come from accounts I am personally familiar with, with real numbers and achievable results and not fictional projections.

Chapter 1

Since the market value in most cases has depended primarily upon the dividend rate, the latter could be held responsible for nearly all the gains realized by investors. (Security Analysis, by Graham, Dodd & Cottle)

Breaking away from the norm:

I think one of the hardest parts of investing is trying to decide how and which advice, because most seems quite sensible, to apply to your own investment strategy:

- Invest in yourself first.
- Stocks are primarily a long-term investment.
- Avoid High Yield Stocks.
- Only make investments you understand.
- Learn from the mistakes of others.
- Consider the level of risk you can accept.
- Keep your investment fees low.

You've probably heard these and many more, most are valid, others sound reasonable but don't really pertain to your particular situation, or leave you wondering how to implement what they advise.

So, what might make investing simpler and practical for you? After many years of playing the market and reading a number of published materials on various investment strategies, I have found that investing for income and concentrating on income growth is the best, most risk-free way to utilize the market. We're not giving up on capital appreciation, just ignoring the constant monitoring of the market's ups and downs.

Every day the financial news announces the markets' movement. On BNN and the CTV News channel, the current price of each stock scrolls across the screen providing updates of their current price and how much the price is up or down for the day. The news anchor and others may have opinions on what's causing the change, and some will provide projections or recommendations on the latest best buys or what to avoid.

The problem with all the news and financial advice is that it's all centered on the changes in the market, the price of stocks and the short-term changes of those stock prices. Whatever happened to investing for the long-term? No wonder the majority of investors panic if the market drops 200 points or more.

So, if one is wary of constant monitoring of the market and its volatility, what's the alternative?

Income is the alternative!

The stock producing the income is worth more as the income it produces increases(Lowell Miller, The Single Best Investment)

So, how do we stop watching the price of stocks or caring if the market is up or down? One of the easiest methods is to change the way you think about your investments and what you expect from them. With this book I would like to convince you that it's not that difficult to concentrate on the concept of "income" and show you how it becomes much easier over time.

When one considers a GIC or bond it's the interest rate that's important. In fact, most people will shop around to find the best or highest interest rate available and after they've bought, they forget about the purchase. The main reason people buy GICs or bonds is because they know they will get back their original capital (investment) plus the interest. But the problem is that the interest is fixed, meaning it stays the same. We said we want a growing income and that we can achieve that goal by investing in stocks which pay and grow their dividend (what I refer to as income).

Apply the same thinking to the stocks you are considering, as you would if they were GICs, but substitute income for interest rate. Ask yourself, how much income your investments are going to return, **but also ask the question, will your income grow**?

Once you are ready to change the way you think about your stocks, we also want to replace the word "price" with "income" and make that your focus. For example, instead of wondering if your stock price(s) are up, check to see if your income is up, and disregard price altogether. It's not that price isn't important, it's just that one should not make it the key focus of your attention. Realize you will be holding your stocks for the long-term. The goal is to find good investments, then give them time to grow the income, which will then, in turn, grow the price.

However, even the staunchest dividend supporters have difficulty getting away from watching price. How often have you heard or read the following comment; "You are getting paid while you wait".

Every time I read or hear someone making that statement, I think, wait for what? What else could they mean but for prices to go up! Even those thinking about income and possibly aware of its benefit are stuck in the same rut, always watching price. Let's see if I can help change that.

Why income?

- Income will make your investment choices easier,
- You will mostly invest in large, stable and profitable companies,
- You will see your income grow each month or quarter,
- Your growing income will also grow the stock price,
- Your income will not be affected by market fluctuations, and
- You will learn to ignore the daily changes in share price and market changes.

To illustrate how income investing works, I will use a real-world example. My wife bought shares of a bank stock for our grandson in 2007 and invested the following amounts:

2007	$ 5,555	(market peak)
2008	$ 500	(financial crisis)
2009	$ 500	(financial crisis)
2011	$ 1,000	(start of recovery)
2017	$ 1,000	(10 years later)
	$ 8,555	(total investment)

The following chart shows the income they received and the income growth rate for each year:

2008	$217.30	
2009	$253.81	16.80%
2010	$281.43	10.88%
2011	$323.94	15.10%
2012	$379.31	17.09%
2013	$431.32	13.71%
2014	$481.32	11.59%
2015	$531.84	10.50%
2016	$588.67	10.69%
2017	$655.52	11.36%
2018	$767.36	17.06%
	$4,911.82	(income received and reinvested)

Look at the rising income each year and how consistent the income growth percentage is each year. Money was not added every year, yet the income continued to grow by at least 10%, over the previous year, regardless of the market fluctuations during that period. Had she put the money in a GIC, at 1% or even 2%, during those years of low rates, how much income would they have received over the 11 years? At such a low rate of return, not much, as well there would have been no real income growth. In our case, by concentrating on dividend growth stocks, the income grew in 11 years from $217.30 to $767.36, or 253.13%!

I will provide another example. My wife (the better stock picker) bought this stock in 2008, at a market high, added funds for a few years and has ignored the stock since 2011.

2007	$ 37	(bought one share)
2008	$10,000	(initial purchase in Jan 08)
2008	$ 5,000	(invested at a high price)
2010	$ 2,500	(added funds)
2011	$ 2,000	(last purchase)
	$19,537	(total investment)

Here's the income she received each year and the annual income growth rate:

2008	$ 286.88	(no pymt 2 Qtr 2008)
2009	$ 634.17	121.06%
2010	$ 788.03	24.26%
2011	$ 936.85	18.89%
2012	$1,066.76	13.87%
2013	$1,159.46	8.69%
2014	$1,257.04	8.42%
2015	$1,398.84	11.28%
2016	$1,584.02	13.24%
2017	$1,813.84	14.51%
2018	$2,091.42	12.30%
	$13,017.31	(income received & reinvested)

This example also shows that my wife has gotten 67% of her initial investment back just from the income she's received ($13,017/19,537) x 100 = 67%. As for income growth, from 2009 (first full year of income) to 2018, the income grew from $634.17/year to $2,091.42/year or 229.79%.

She's essentially being "paid" while she waits, but not for the stock price to rise, but rather, for her next income payment to increase.

In both examples most of the investment in the stocks were made before the financial crisis (meaning we paid a high price for the stocks before the market dropped in 2009), but they have averaged 10% income growth each year and above. Even with severe market fluctuations, the benefits of income growth investing are real and substantial. Remember, with income investing we are not watching the price of the stocks, but the income those stocks provide.

And this is what I want you to understand. By investing in "income-earning" stocks (which I will discuss later in this book), you will see your income grow each year regardless of how much you invest, whether the market is up or down, even if you stop adding funds to your holdings. Of course, your income will grow faster the more you invest, but the ultimate goal is always income growth. Did I forget to mention price? No, because our eyes are on the income.

So, are you ready? Let's get started.

Chapter 2

Do not save what is left after spending, but spend what is left after saving. (Warren Buffett, Chairman and CEO, Berkshire Hathaway)

The first step:

Before one can generate income, one must begin saving money. The savings do not have to be large, in the beginning, but should be made on a regular basis and increase as one earns more. Whether you start saving $50 a month or $1,000 a month, saving as a priority is the beginning of any successful investment strategy. You must save money to make money and the more you save the more you make.

A great philosophy for saving is to not think about it, instead, make it a routine!

I also suggest you reduce your debt and avoid any payments where excessive interest is being charged, such as credit cards. A Loan Consolidation is one way to reduce the cost of interest, **provided you don't start adding additional debt**.

There are some excellent books and reference sources available to help people to reduce debt and cut expenses, probably better advice than I can provide (consider "How not to move back in with your parents: the young person's complete guide to financial empowerment", by Rob Carrick). Regardless of your current financial health, one must make the effort to save and then not touch your investment money, even for short-term needs.

Let's get back to business, once you have decided you are ready to start saving you may be ready to start investing.

Many beginner investors put their money into High Interest Savings accounts or GIC's, and that's fine, **but don't consider savings and investments as the same thing.** Everyone should have a cash reserve and savings which might be used to cover unexpected expenses. But your investments should be considered future money, a **Retirement Time Capsule** if you will, which should not be touched until you need it in retirement.

Whether you start investing at age 20 or 60 will not affect the strategy I propose. What will change is how you choose to invest (I will discuss the choices later in the book) and of course, the amounts you can invest. Obviously, someone starting at 20 years old will not have large amounts to invest but does have the advantage of time, time for their investments to grow and compound. Someone who starts later, even as late as 60 years old, will need to invest larger amounts and have a shorter timeline before they will begin to draw down funds. Still, even 10 years can provide significant income from a large portfolio of income producing stocks, as I'll demonstrate later in the book.

If you are not investing for income, then it is fair to analyze or ask, what they expect of their savings during retirement. Is it a guaranteed fixed income, their capital to be secure, perhaps just the ability to sell a portion of the capital to meet their needs (the 4% withdrawal is often suggested)? And of course, they hope not to outlive their money. But how often have you heard someone say, "I want to enjoy my retirement while I can and die broke"? Too many in my experience.

The sad part is that many might get their wish, by finding during their retirement years they must cut expenses and curb their lifestyle to make ends meet. Nothing is more stressful in retirement then feeling you might outlive your financial resources!

I'd prefer to have my investments generate an ever-growing income stream, one which continues to grow, especially during retirement, while I'm drawing down funds.

It is important to remember that when interest rates dropped during the financial crisis of 2008-2009, so did the interest paid on fixed income (GIC's and Bonds). In fact, they almost dropped to zero. The value of stocks fell as well, so those depending upon selling shares and fixed income to meet their daily expenses found they had little or no protection and most likely suffered profound losses. Luckily, during that period and after several years of low interest rates, inflation remained at 1.5% to 2%. Small comfort.

Inflation: up, up and up!

Inflation is a rise in the general level of prices of goods and services in an economy over a period of time. When the general price level rises, each unit of currency buys fewer goods and services. Consequently, inflation also reflects an erosion in the purchasing power of money – a loss of real value in the internal medium of exchange and unit of account in the economy. A chief measure of price inflation is the inflation rate, the annualized percentage change in a general price index normally the Consumer Price Index over time.

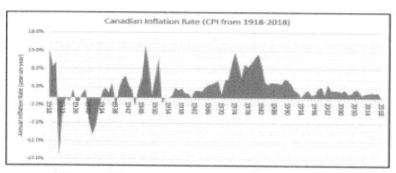

Data sourced from Canada's annual Consumer Price Index by Statistics Canada (StatCan).
"CA$100 in 1942 → 2018 | Canada Inflation Calculator." U.S. Official Inflation Data, Alioth
Finance, 25 Nov. 2018,

Year	Canadian Inflation Rate	CAD Value
1998	1.00%	$ 971
1999	2.63%	$ 997
2000	3.20%	$ 1,029
2001	0.72%	$ 1,036
2002	3.80%	$ 1,076
2003	2.08%	$ 1,098
2004	2.13%	$ 1,121
2005	2.09%	$ 1,145
2006	1.67%	$ 1,164
2007	2.38%	$ 1,191
2008	1.16%	$ 1,205
2009	1.32%	$ 1,221
2010	2.35%	$ 1,250
2011	2.30%	$ 1,279
2012	0.83%	$ 1,289
2013	1.24%	$ 1,305
2014	1.47%	$ 1,324
2015	1.61%	$ 1,346
2016	1.50%	$ 1,366
2017	1.56%	$ 1,387
2018	2.22%	$ 1,418

Since 1918 through 2018, inflation rate dropped only twelve times, but for every other year the price of goods and services has increased. The last time inflation dropped was 1952. The graph is misleading, because the increases in inflation compound every year. This means that what cost a dollar one year, cost more the next and even more the next. The average inflation rate since 1918 has been2.9% per year, meaning prices double every 25 years (looking at the chart on the right, you will see that what cost $971 in 1998 now costs $1,418 in 2018, up 46.04% in 20 years). I always question those figures because many essential items seem to have increased much faster than the reported rate of increase.

In the Lee Child novels his character, Jack Reacher, often says, "Hope for the best, but plan for the worst". Apply that rule to inflation and hope that inflation remains low or below average, but plan for much higher-inflation and costs.

Ultimately this is my goal, to recommend a way for your investments to provide a growing stream of income to offset rising costs. Not a "pie in the sky" or "jackpot at the end of a rainbow" goal, but a simple method where you see the results of your efforts as time goes on and feel confident that your **"Retirement Time Capsule"** will meet your future income needs.

Visionary

Most people don't consider themselves as visionary: "thinking about or planning the future with imagination or wisdom".

I think you have the opportunity to become a visionary about your financial future, but thinking or planning about it won't get you there. One has to work to achieve their dreams and I believe the Income Growth investment strategy can help make your dreams a reality.

Chapter 3

A careful selection of a few investments having regard to...their potential intrinsic value over a period of years ahead and...a steadfast holding of these fairly large units through thick and thin. (John Maynard Keynes, British Economist, creator of Keynesian economics)

Getting schooled:

Once you've started saving for your future, I suggest the next step is to develop an investment strategy. Here you have lots of choices, but where to start and which to choose? Do I start buying stocks and try to sell when they rise 15%? Do I follow BNN Market Call and select their recommended 3 Picks? Do I buy a group of Exchange Traded Funds (ETF) and hope for market returns, or do I try to figure out how to start a Value or Growth portfolio because my ultimate goal is to beat the market return? That's the problem many investors face and, unfortunately, the majority will lose money trying to make guesswork their market strategy. Yes, money can be made, it has been done, but those that succeed will often be a small minority.

The Income Growth Investment Strategy:

Dividend paying ability, in the long run, determines value. (Arnold Bernhard, founder of Value Line).

Income investing could be considered the flip side of "growing the pile" (having the value of your investments go up). Most investors consider the combination of capital appreciation (stocks going up in price) and dividends (see Definitions) as their total return. However, too many consider dividends as the minor contributor of the two.

I believe the exact opposite. I believe that dividends (what I refer to as income), especially a growing dividend, is the driver that generates price growth and, in the end, contributes to a more sustainable return.

A dividend is derived from a company's earnings. If a company is growing its earnings and paying out an ever-higher amount in dividends, eventually investors will recognize the value of those higher dividends and begin buying the shares. Subsequently, the price of those shares will rise.

Investing for income (dividends) means you will look for companies that pay you dividends for buying and holding their shares. **To achieve a growing income, the company should increase the dividend over time, thereby providing you with more income for each share you own, and not requiring you to sell shares to receive the higher income.**

Your income will be generated from holding "individual" stocks, not a bundle (i.e. Exchange Traded Funds) which will most likely include mediocre stocks. My strategy works when you hold only quality equities with at least 10 years of positive growing earnings and a history of passing along a percentage of those earnings to the shareholder.

To better illustrate what I call "the income-growth game", I'll compare it to playing golf:

- You don't hit the longest ball but will always be down the middle and in the fairway.
- You don't make headlines for great shots but will continue to play steadily and dependably.
- You probably won't get the occasional Eagle but will consistently get pars and birdies, finding your handicap gradually improving (your income rising).
- You won't be recognized as the #1 player but you will almost always be in the top 10.

I hope that these kinds of odds are ones you are interested in playing. It's not often you truly get exposed to a "sure thing", but in investing, quality dividend growth stocks come as close as you can get!

Why not just buy an ETF?

Bullet-proof, dividend paying common stocks with a record of sustained payout growth should be the core investment asset class for income-oriented investors. (Don Coxe, Basic Points, Sept. 2011)

ETFs (Exchange Traded Funds) are fast becoming the choice of many investors. They are a way to have a diversified portfolio of stocks or bonds in a single investment and can be traded just like a stock. The fees are low and they offer vast diversification, a way to "cover all the bases", if you will. Some suggest that if you own around three to five ETFs, you'll cover the entire Canadian, US, Emerging and International markets. However, there are now about 22 Canadian ETF Providers and 495 ETFs available to choose from, with new ETFs coming out almost weekly. Considering ETFs can contain hundreds, if not thousands of individual stocks, it is no longer a simple choice, is it?

Let me say that there is no best method to invest and ETFs may be a reasonable choice for those who have set market returns as their objective. But, from an "income" perspective, I do have a few objections to them, mainly because:

- They hold too many stocks, the good, bad and in-between, which must result in average or lower income and returns,
- The distribution (Income) rarely grows or grows at a slow rate,
- The distribution may include dividends, Return of Capital, and Capital Gains, misleading investors who assume the distribution is all dividends,
- Although ETFs initial fees may appear to be low, the more you invest the higher the fees become,
- You have no control over the stocks chosen or their weighting within the ETF (for example, one stock may be 3.5%, while another .05%),
- The fund needs to trade (constant buying and selling) to rebalance,
- If you were to use our 4 Rules (discussed later) to evaluate all the stocks in a single ETF, you would most likely find many of them to be poor or mediocre performers as dividend growth stocks, and
- Most ETFs try to match the performance to the market or Index they represent. Since the financial crisis of 2008, the market has generally been on an upswing. But I do wonder how ETFs will do during

the next major correction or extended sideways market. Personally, I do not think they will do well.

Remember, that if our objective is long-term income growth, you will find that ETFs don't provide the income growth that individual stocks do. I will be explaining further and support my hesitation to recommend ETFs with some facts when I provide my stock evaluation process.

As for the various other investment choices, they are all dependent on price and the market, which is what we are attempting to avoid.

Which stocks and where to find them?

Investors should remain focused on high-quality investments such as strong dividend-paying stocks and use volatility to their advantage. (David Rosenberg, Journalist, *Financial Post*)

I have already mentioned that I like dividend-paying stocks, and in Canada it's not too hard to find them. Still, wouldn't it be great to have a process to help us confirm their quality?

The Canadian TSX Index lists about 3800 stocks and the TSX 60 Index (see Appendix A) consists of the 60 largest companies that trade on the TSX Exchange. These are the companies I want you to stick with: the large, profitable companies that pay dividends. Most of the stocks in the TSX 60 Index are dividend-payers, **but it is important to remember there are dividend-payers, and then there are dividend-growth payers.**

This is an important distinction because if a company does not raise their dividend than your income will not grow and compound at an accelerated rate (I'll provide examples later in the book). And, that is the backbone of my strategy. We want to find companies which have grown their dividend on a consistent basis and for many, many years. We want to screen out the stocks which do not grow their dividend.

My strategy is not flashy. Nor is it about getting rich quick. The companies that you may find most suitable with my method may not be the fastest growing, highest flyers, but should provide you with a steady stream of income and, most importantly, grow that income at a reasonable rate as time goes on. This is what generates reliable income so you can ignore market fluctuation and share price.

In addition, a company's status changes over time. What were quality dividend growth stocks 8 to 10 years ago, may not qualify today. They may still be good companies which pay and grow their dividend but may not meet the requirements to be considered good stocks to buy today. **But Income investing is more than just a growing dividend, which we discuss later.** *

Excel worksheets:

Before we evaluate each of the TSX 60 stocks, I want to suggest, if you are not already familiar with Excel, I hope you will explore using it, or at least a similar program.

Besides providing more information than what your broker (from whom you purchase stocks) offers, it is a very efficient method to observe greater detail on your holdings. Excel also performs many calculations easily, such as calculating the 75% dividend growth rate or the 10-year average dividend yield of each stock, the adjusted cost base (average cost) of each stock, the

35

annual dividend income growth, current yield and yield on your total investment percentages and growth, all of which we will discuss later.

I should point out that a disadvantage of Excel is that you need to cross-check your data to ensure the numbers and report balances shown in Excel are correct. You should always check your Excel balance and number of shares with your broker's account balances. But even with its limitations, Excel will enable you to design specific reports to provide the information you wish or would like to see, I feel strongly any investment strategy benefits from diligent data tracking.

Whatever method you use, I feel you will begin to look forward to tracking your progress.

You can download the sample Excel package from:

https://drive.google.com/drive/u/1/folders/1kD-ZtK7WkIINobzB3HYJ1tnwnh9P3NDf

The download will include the following worksheet (formulas included), where you'll record your evaluation results for each stock and add useful comments. This tracking is an integral part of an income growth investment strategy.

Symbol	Div Cuts Yes/No	Pd Div 10Yrs Yes/No	Raised Div 10yrs Yes/No	Start Div	Ending Div	Div Gth 75% over 10yrs	Current Yield	Consider Purchase Yes/No and Comments
AEM								
ATD.B								
ARX								
BMO								
BNS								
BCE								

I'll describe what the headings are and where to find the information in the next section.

So, let's get started and "sort the wheat from the chaff".

Jumping the stocks through the hoops:

Know what you own and know why you own it. (Peter Lynch, manager of the Magellan Fund)

As I've said before, not all dividend growth stocks are created equal, and after my own successes and failures at "stock picking" I began to direct my research specifically to figure out just how to minimize risk and maximize results. If, like me, you've read other investing books, you may wonder how anyone could simplify the process of selecting and evaluating stocks. Well, you are in for a surprise, because I found it to be so simple, I wonder why everyone does not do it.

The steps are so simple, that if you answer "yes" to the very first question on any stock you're researching, then you do not need to proceed further. The stock would be immediately eliminated as a quality dividend growth (DG) stock. The other three questions can be considered guidelines and are not as fixed as the first.

The Four Guiding Rules:

1. Has the company cut their dividend in the past 10 years, Yes or No?
2. Has the company paid a dividend for a minimum of 10 years (25 or more is even better)?
3. Has the company had a consistent record of raising their dividend for 10 years (The more often the increase, the better the stock).
4. Has the dividend grown over the past 10 years by at least 75%?

The first rule is fixed because companies that cut their dividend are either a cyclical stock or it's a sign that the company has had financial problems. We want to avoid cyclical stocks because we are seeking reliable income from the companies we choose. If the company has financial problems, it will likely take many years before it recovers.

If a company has not cut their dividend and you answer "yes" to the other three questions, I suggest you add the company to a new list, which I like to call your "**List of Stocks to Consider**". I emphasize the word "consider", as this list needs to be flexible and monitored periodically, as it is likely to change over time. The list is intended to be your "buy" list.

Many may feel that rules are not meant to be broken, but there are valid exceptions and I'd like you to remember, **if you are not flexible you risk becoming outdated**.

To illustrate my point, let's look at three different "exception" scenarios:

1. **A company has paid and raised their dividend for 10 years, but the dividend growth is less than 75%.**
   This is an example of an exception because there are companies, like utilities, that have raised their dividend for many years, I like to call them the "Steady Eddies". Many of them post a 5% dividend increase over 10 years which provides a 63% dividend growth, below our 75%, but I still consider them an attractive stock choice.

   One must also consider that in the event of the financial crisis and low interest rates the dividend growth rates have slowed for many companies. This kind of fluctuation should not necessarily cancel a good long-time performing stock from your list. Regardless of my example, you will have to consider the situation and decide if you wish to add the company with a lower dividend growth rate to your list.

2. **A company has only paid a dividend for 8 or 9 years (which is less than the 10-year minimum), but posts a better-than 75% growth.**
There are plenty of examples of a company paying a dividend for less than the ideal 10-year minimum time period, raising their dividend yearly and posting a growth rate at or above 75%. (By less than 10-year, I mean between 8 and 9 years. Any less would be too short a time period for serious consideration). These companies might be considered new dividend growers and should be looked at seriously.

3. **A company has paid a dividend for 10 years, but not grown the dividend each year (perhaps, 7 of 10 years) and has a lower than 75% dividend growth rate.**
Most Canadian banks are examples of this exception. In 2008 they were discouraged from raising their dividend until their financial reserves were higher. Beyond this development, and for many years before, their growth was steady, their dividend payout and dividend increase exceptional. My experience with Canadian bank stocks is that they are secure long-term dividend growth investments.

*Note: I am providing these "exception rules" as I don't want you to overlook a good company just because it currently does not meet all my guidelines. Still, each stock fitting into one of the three exceptions should be assessed individually, in the end, it is up to you to determine your comfort level in eliminating them or not.

Web sources to find the data

There are several sources I will recommend to find the dividend data we'll use to evaluate the stocks. Morningstar is our first choice and to access the data you should Sign Up, but just for the "Free Access" rather than the Premium services.

Once you've registered and Logged-In, you will be able to access the data by following steps listed in the next section.

I will also list other sources to obtain the dividend data and provide you with step-by-step procedures to enter the data into the Excel worksheets.

How to apply the four rules: Using Morningstar and Yahoo

Login into Morningstar website:
https://members.morningstar.ca/login.aspx#334-hidenews

Enter the stock symbol, I'll use ARX, for ARC Resources

Record the Forward Div Yield onto your TSX60 stock worksheet.

Next click "Key Ratios", then "Full Key Ratio Data"

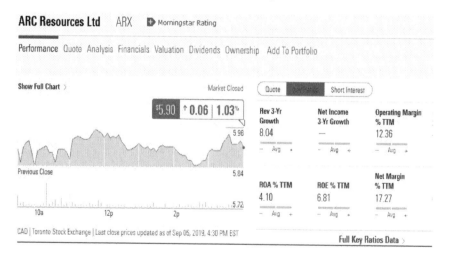

You will then see more company data and the Dividends listed for the past 10 years. Record the beginning and endings dividend on your Excel "TSX60 Wkst". The 10yr dividend Growth percentage will automatically be calculated.

ARC Resources Ltd ARX | ★★★★

Financials

Export 🗗 | Ascending

	2009-12	2010-12	2011-12	2012-12	2013-12	2014-12	2015-12	2016-12	2017-12	2018-12
Revenue CAD M	842	1,214	1,438	1,389	1,624	2,107	1,194	1,564	1,726	1,505
Gross Margin %	68.5	60.1	61.7	41.6	48.4	45.5	-6.0	43.1	49.3	45.3
Operating Income CAD M	218	176	285	147	340	457	-498	46	225	237
Operating Margin %	25.9	14.5	19.8	10.6	20.9	21.7	-41.8	4.3	18.4	15.8
Net Income CAD M	223	261	287	189	340	381	-342	201	398	234
Earnings Per Share CAD	0.36	0.80	1.00	0.47	0.77	1.20	-1.01	0.57	1.10	0.60
Dividends CAD	1.38	1.20	1.20	1.30	1.20	1.30	1.20	0.65	0.60	0.60

Name	Symbol	Div Cuts Yes/No	Pd Div 10Yrs Yes/No	Raised Div 10yrs Yes/No	Start Div	Ending Div	Div Gth 75% over 10yrs	Current Yield	Consider Purchase Yes/No and Comments
Barrick Gold Corp	ABX	Yes	Yes	No	0.40	0.12	-70.00%	0.99%	No, Div Cut
Agnico Eagle Mines Limited	AEM	Yes	Yes	No	0.18	0.44	144.44%	0.83%	No, Div not selling see Pd Gth
Arc Resources Ltd	ARX	Yes	Yes	No	1.28	0.60	-53.13%	10.17%	No, 4 Div Cuts

Just by looking at the 10-year dividends: ARX paid **1.28, 1.20**, 1.20, 1.30, **1.20**, 1.20, 1.20, **0.65, 0.60** and 0.60, you can see that they have cut the dividend four times (in bold).This automatically eliminates ARX from consideration, but record the numbers and your comments on the TSX60 worksheet.

For the next example, let's look up BCE. Follow the sames steps to get to the data.

1. BCEs 10-year dividends were 1.58, 1.78, 2.04, 2.22, 2.33, 2.47, 2.60, 2.73, 2.87 and 3.02. They had no dividend cuts, paid a dividend for 10 years, and raised the dividend each year thereby qualifying for 3 of 4 questions of our four-rule test.

BCE Inc BCE | ★★★★

Last Price	Day Change		Open Price	Day Range	52-Week Range	Yield	Market Cap
$56.22	↑0.23 | 0.41%		$ 55.51	55.50-56.23	50.72-61.89	5.39%	50.5 bil

After Hours : 56.05 -0.17| -0.30%
As of Fri 14/12/2018 4:16 PM EST | CAD
BATS BZX Real-Time Price

Volume	Avg Vol.	Forward P/E	Price/Book Price/Sales Price/
1.3 mil	1.8 mil	15.4	3.0 2.2 Flow
			6.9

BETA Quote Analyst Report Chart Shareholders Financials Insiders Performance | Key Stats | Valuation Filings

Financials

Export   Ascending

	2008-12	2009-12	2010-12	2011-12	2012-12	2013-12	2014-12	2015-12	2016-12	2017-12
Revenue CAD Mil	17,698	17,735	18,069	19,497	19,975	20,400	21,042	21,514	21,719	22,719
Gross Margin %	75.0	74.5	72.6	39.1	48.9	48.8	48.5	48.4	49.3	49.5
Operating Income CAD Mil	3,735	3,718	3,896	3,959	4,495	4,709	4,851	5,131	5,260	5,328
Operating Margin %	21.1	21.0	21.6	20.3	22.5	23.1	23.1	23.8	24.3	23.5
Net Income CAD Mil	943	1,738	2,277	2,340	2,763	2,106	2,500	2,678	3,031	2,914
Earnings Per Share CAD	1.01	2.11	2.74	2.88	3.17	2.54	2.97	2.98	3.33	3.11
Dividends CAD	0.73	1.58	1.78	2.04	2.22	2.33	2.47	2.60	2.73	2.87
Payout Ratio % *	65.2	74.5	62.6	71.4	65.5	77.4	81.9	85.0	85.3	87.8

Source Morningstar

2. When you enter the beginning and ending dividend on the TSX60 worksheet the 10yr dividend growth percentage is shown. The starting dividend is 1.58 and it ended at 3.02 in 2018, so (3.02-1.58)/1.58 x 100 = 91.14%. This shows a percentage above the 75% dividend growth rate, so BCE passes all four-rule tests and should be added to your "**List of Stocks to Consider**".

Follow the same process to find and enter the dividend data for the remaining TSX 60 stocks and record your findings on the TSX60 Stock worksheet. I suggest you keep the data for all the stocks you analyze, even adding extra comments and impressions, regardless of purchase. It is very useful to track stock performance of all companies, it usually confirms, with a quick glance, why you would purchase, or not, any stock. I have provided a few more examples of how I applied the four-rule tests with AEM, ATD.B, BMO, and BNS on the chart below, this should give you a good idea of how the Excel spreadsheet works within the process.

Name	Symbol	Div Cuts Yes/No	Pd Div 10Yrs Yes/No	Raised Div 10yrs Yes/No	Start Div	Ending Div	Div Gth 75% over 10yrs	Current Yield	Consider Purchase Yes/No and Comments
Barrick Gold Corp	ABX	Yes	Yes	No	0.40	0.12	-70.00%	0.89%	No, Div Cut
Agnico Eagle Mines Limited	AEM	Yes	Yes	No	0.18	0.44	144.44%		No, Div Cut
Arc Resources Ltd	ARX	Yes	Yes	No	1.28	0.60	-53.13%		No, Div Cut
Alimentation Couche-Tard	ATD.B	No	Yes	Yes	0.05	0.32	540.00%		Yes, Good Div Growth
Brookfield Asset Management	BAM.A	No	Yes	No	0.35	0.60	71.43%		No, but maybe exception
Blackberry Limited	BB						#DIV/0!		No, no div paid
Bombardier Inc Cl. B Sv	BBD.B						#DIV/0!		No, no div paid
BCE Inc	BCE	No	Yes	Yes	1.58	3.02	91.14%	5.35%	Yes, steady Gth, watch payout ratio
Bausch Health Companies Inc	BHC						#DIV/0!		No, no div paid
CGI Group Inc Cl.A Sv	GIB.A						#DIV/0!		No, no div paid
Bank of Montreal	BMO	No	Yes	No	2.80	3.78	35.00%		No, Low Div Gth
Bank of Nova Scotia	BNS	No	Yes	No 9 of 10	1.96	3.28	67.35%		Yes, Exception
Ccl Industries Inc Cl. B Nv	CCL.B	No	Yes	Yes	0.12	0.52	333.33%		Yes, good Gth

This exercise is important because this book is not intended to provide you with a list of recommended stocks to choose from. I would rather provide you with the tools, a process by which to gather and analyze the data, so that you can come to your own conclusions and make your own decisions. Once you become comfortable with this method of evaluation, you can apply it to any stock, or any index.

I liken my four-rule test to a "Dividend Growth Sluice". To separate out the cyclical, low-quality and low growth stocks, to be left with those few gems, the dividend growth payers!

Calculating 10 Year Average Yields

For just the stocks that you feel pass the Four-Rule test, I now suggest you calculate the 10-year average yield percentages. Morningstar only provided 5 years of Trailing Yield percentages, so to calculate the 10-year Average yield for any of the TSX 60 stocks, or others, I obtain the information from Yahoo Finance.

You need to record the 10-year dividends paid from Morningstar onto the "AveYld" Excel worksheet.

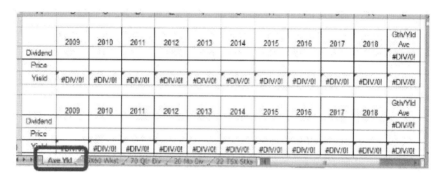

For this sample I'll use BCE. We will have already gotten the dividend paid each year from Morningstar, so we need only obtain the price to use at the end of each year. Actually, I'm going to use the price just after the dividend was paid.

Let's go to the Yahoo website:

https://ca.finance.yahoo.com/quote/%5EGSPTSE/history/

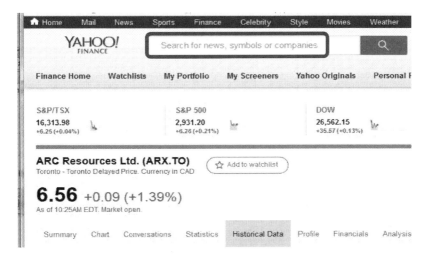

1. Enter the Symbol, in this case BCE.TO and search
2. Click Historical Data
3. Click the Dates by the Time Period and enter they beginning year you wish, I'm using 1/01/2009:

4. Change the Frequency to **"Monthly"**, then click **"Apply"**

5. Arrow down to the last dividend paid in 2009

Jan. 01, 2010	28.09	28.13	25.68	25.75
Dec. 11, 2009				0.405 Dividend
Dec. 01, 2009	26.76	27.68	24.67	27.61

6. Record the price shown just above the dividend (the fourth number) or $25.75 and record the figure on the "AveYld" Price cell for 2009.

BCE	2009	2010	2011	2012	2013	2014	2015	2016	2017	2018	Gth/Yld Ave
Dividend	1.58	1.78	2.04	2.22	2.33	2.47	2.6	2.73	2.87	3.02	91.14%
Price	25.75										
Yield	6.14%	#DIV/0!	#DIV/0!	#DIV/0!	#DIV/0!	#DIV/0!	#DIV/0!	#DIV/0!	#DIV/0!	#DIV/0!	#DIV/0!

7. Arrow up to find the last dividend paid for 2010 and record the price, in the fourth column, on your worksheet. Continue to record each year closing price.

8. When finished the yearly yields will be shown and the Averge Yield for the 10 years, in this case 5.75%, as will the dividend growth for the 10 years, 91.14%.

BCE	2009	2010	2011	2012	2013	2014	2015	2016	2017	2018	Gth/Yld Ave
Dividend	1.58	1.78	2.04	2.22	2.33	2.47	2.60	2.73	2.87	3.02	91.14%
Price	25.75	36.33	40.80	44.42	41.97	45.95	40.30	45.12	46.75	43.50	
Yield	6.14%	4.90%	5.00%	5.00%	5.55%	5.38%	6.45%	6.05%	6.14%	6.94%	5.75%

9. Follow the same process, using the Morningstar dividend data and Yahoo price data to calculate the Dividend Growth % and the Average Yield % for stock you wish. There are plenty of company blank data on the AveYld worksheet.

10. *Remember to save the worksheet. I suggest you use "Save As" giving the worksheet a new name, such as 2019 Stock Analysis or 2019 My Stock Worksheet. Every time you update or change the data re-save immediately.

Summarizing your data

Now we can summarize the data we've collected for all the stocks which passed our Four-Rule test onto the "List of Stocks to Consider" worksheet, entering the required data.

List of Stocks to Consider			Start Div	Ending Div	10 Yr Div Gth%	10 Yr Ave Yield	Current Div	Current Price	Current Yield
Bank of Nova Scotia	BNS	Bank	1.96	3.28	67.35%	3.97%	3.48	$71.91	4.84%
BCE	BCE	Commun	1.58	3.02	91.14%	4.94%	3.17	$63.37	5.00%

On the right side I've added some columns with Suggested Buy Price, three of them. By entering a Price, it will calculate the Yield in the next column. By enter three different prices you will see the yields you will receive at buy at those prices. By reviewing the yields and comparing them to the 10-year average yield for the stock, you'll see if you will get a reasonable yield if purchased.

For example, I'll enter three prices for BNS and BCE:

10 Yr Ave Yield	Current Div	Current Price	Current Yield	Suggested Buy Price	Yield %	Suggested Buy Price	Yield %	Suggested Buy Price	Yield %
3.97%	3.48	$71.91	4.84%	$67.00	5.19%	$66.50	5.23%	$66.00	5.27%
4.94%	3.17	$63.37	5.00%	$63.90	5.45%	$63.45	5.48%	$63.00	5.52%

I entered $67, $66.50 and $66 for BNS, which provides yields of 5.19%, 5.23% and 5.27%, while the 10-year average yield is 3.79%, all three prices offer yields above the 10 yr. average. You can see the BCE figures as well.

2nd. Alternative for dividend data

The next section is the Alternative source for the dividend history, using The Dividend Channel. You will need to download the "Sample Reports Cdn New" worksheet because it contains the 70 QtrDiv (70 Quarterly dividend paying companies) and 20 Mo Div (20 Monthly dividend paying companies) worksheet which will be used to copy the data for each company from:

https://drive.google.com/drive/u/1/folders/1kD-ZtK7WkIINobzB3HYJ1tnwnh9P3NDf

How to apply the four rules: Using the Dividend Channel

Go to The Dividend Channel online: https

In the box "Enter Symbol" type the company symbol, but add

.CA for any Canadian stock or fund.

Type in the first company symbol you want to evaluate in the box Fund/Stock at the top that you wish to research. I'll use ARX for ARC Resources, as my example.

Arrow down till you see the Dividend History on the right side:

DIVIDEND HISTORY	
Date	**Div***
06/27/19	0.050
05/30/19	0.050
04/29/19	0.050
03/28/19	0.050
02/27/19	0.050
01/30/19	0.050
12/28/18	0.050
11/29/18	0.050
10/30/18	0.050

The Dividend Channel list the dividends paid by month or quarter. It does not total them by year. You can add up the dividends and enter the yearly total in the "AveYld" worksheet or follow the steps below to copy the data into a worksheet.

Here comes the tricky part for some, as you will need to copy the data from the website onto the Sample worksheet.

With Excel open, click the Tab 70 QtrDiv, for companies which pay quarterly dividends or the Tab 20 Mo Div for those which pay monthly dividends. You open them by clicking the Tab at the bottom of the TSX 60 worksheet.

Quarterly Dividends		Monthly Dividends	
12/13/2018	0.755	12/28/2018	0.05
9/13/2018	0.755	11/29/2018	0.05
6/14/2018	0.755	10/30/2018	0.05
3/14/2018	0.755	9/27/2018	0.05
12/14/2017	0.718	8/30/2018	0.05
70 Qtr Div / 20 Mo Div		70 Qtr Div / 20 Mo Div	

Here are the steps to copy 10 years of Dividend History and insert the data into the Excel worksheet

1. We will work from the latest full year dividends, in this case it's 2018, so we will ignore the 2019 payments and start with Dec 28, 2018 for ARX

2. **Left Click, and Hold** the left mouse button down on the 12/28/2018 and

DIVIDEND HISTORY	
Date	**Div**
06/27/19	0.050
05/30/19	0.050
04/29/19	0.050
03/28/19	0.050
02/27/19	0.050
01/30/19	0.050
12/28/18	0.050
11/29/18	0.050
10/30/18	0.050
09/27/18	0.050
08/30/18	0.050

3. **Drag the mouse down** to the dividends paid for 10 years, which will be the first payment of 2009 (Jan 28 2009 for ARX)

06/26/09	0.100
05/27/09	0.100
04/28/09	0.120
03/27/09	0.120
02/25/09	0.120
01/28/09	0.120
12/29/08	0.150
11/26/08	0.200

4. If you go past the Jan 2009 date, move the mouse back up, not releasing the Left mouse button *If you **don't get the section highlighted you will have to try again.**

5. When you have the Jan 28 2009 date and dividend paid highlighted release the Left mouse button.

6. To copy the data highlighted, Hold the "Ctrl" button down and press the letter "C". **Ctrl C is copy.**

7. Go to the Excel worksheet and open the 20 Mo Div worksheet as ARXs dividend is monthly

8. Click on the cell to the right of Copy Data > and below Monthly Dividends and

Monthly Dividends

Copy Data >

9. Hold the "Ctrl" key and press "V". **Ctrl V is to paste**.

	Monthly Dividends	
Copy Data >	12/28/2018	0.05
	11/29/2018	0.05
	10/30/2018	0.05
	9/27/2018	0.05
	8/30/2018	0.05
	7/30/2018	0.05
	6/28/2018	0.05
	5/30/2018	0.05
	4/27/2018	0.05
	3/28/2018	0.05
	2/27/2018	0.05
	1/30/2018	0.05	0.60

10. This worksheet allows for 20 Monthly companies (70 companies for Quarterly Dividends) to be entered. Each is listed below the first, so you would arrow down to the next section for the next company paying a monthly dividend.

11. The data will be summarized above with the 10 yr.

ARX	29-Dec-09	29-Dec-10	28-Dec-11	27-Dec-12	27-Dec-13	29-Dec-14	29-Dec-15	28-Dec-16	28-Dec-17	28-Dec-18	10 Yr Gth%
Dividend	1.28	1.20	1.20	1.20	1.20	1.20	1.20	0.65	0.60	0.60	-53.13%
Div Gth Yr		-6.25%	0.00%	0.00%	0.00%	0.00%	0.00%	-45.83%	-7.69%	0.00%	
Price											10yr Ave Yld
Yield %	#DIV/0!	#DIV/0!	#DIV/0!	#DIV/0!	#DIV/0!	#DIV/0!	#DIV/0!	#DIV/0!	#DIV/0!	#DIV/0!	#DIV/0!
Current Yld	#DIV/0!										

DivGth calculated:

Note: If you feel you need to record dividend data for more than 70 quarterly and 20 monthly companies, you can copy either of the worksheets into a new worksheet. Here's how:

1. Click at the top left of the 70 or 20 worksheet

	A	B	C	D	E	
1	Comp Symb >	BCE	11-Dec-09	13-Dec-10	13-Dec-11	12
2		Dividend	1.58	1.79	2.05	
3		Div Gth Yr		13.04%	14.61%	
4						
5		Price	27.47	36.37	40.88	
6		Yield %	5.75%	4.91%	5.01%	
7		Current Yld	5.29%			
8						
9		**Quarterly Dividends**				
10	Copy Data >	12/13/2018	0.755			
11		9/13/2018	0.755			
12		6/14/2018	0.755			

   The space next to A and up from 1

2. By clicking it you will highlight the entire worksheet. Now hold down Ctrl key and press C (**Ctrl C is to copy**)

3. At the bottom click the tab Sheet 1

14	12/14/2017	0.718	
15	9/14/2017	0.718	
16	6/13/2017	0.718	
17	3/13/2017	0.718	2.872

70 Qtr Div / 20 Mo Div / 22 TSX Stks / 26 NOBL Stks / Sheet1

Ready   Count

4. This will open up a new worksheet, and then hold the Ctrl key down and press V (**Ctrl V to paste**).

5. You will now have a duplicate of the 70 QtrDiv or 20 Mo Div worksheet you copied.

6. You can Rename the worksheet by pressing your Right mouse key on Sheet 1 then press the Left mouse key on Rename. Now type what you want to name the worksheet

7. You can repeat the process if you want to do the same for the other worksheet.

3rd. Alternative for dividend data

Dividend Growth Investing & Retirement website

If one signs up (free) at the Dividend Growth Investing & Retirement website (see Appendix C) you can download the Canadian Dividend All-Star List (which is updated periodically). The dividend listing goes back to 2002 for those companies that have paid and raised their dividend five or more years consecutively. This list is very useful because lists companies by the longest number of years that they have raised their dividend.

Canadian Dividend All-Star List

http://www.dividendgrowthinvestingandretirement.com/canadian-divide June 28th

Seq	Ticker	Company	Streak	Price
1	CU.TO	Canadian Utilities	47	$ 36.96
2	FTS.TO	Fortis Inc	45	$ 51.71
3	TIH.TO	Toromont Industries Ltd	29	$ 62.07
4	CWB.TO	Canadian Western Bank	27	$ 29.87
5	ACO-X.TO	Atco Ltd., Cl.I,	25	$ 44.14
6	TRI.TO	Thomson Reuters	25	$ 84.48
		Div in USD, so yiel adj @ 1 USD = 1.3		
7	EMP-A.TO	Empire Company Ltd	24	$ 32.98
8	IMO.TO	Imperial Oil	24	$ 36.26
9	MRU.TO	Metro Inc	24	$ 49.14
10	CNR.TO	Canadian National Railway	23	$ 121.20
11	ENB.TO	Enbridge Inc	23	$ 47.30

When you open the excel file, **arrow way right** till you see the years with the annual dividends listed, as shown below.

Company	2018	2017	2016	2015	2014	2013
Canadian Utilities	$ 1.5732	$ 1.4300	$ 1.3000	$ 1.1800	$ 1.0700	$ 0.9700
Fortis Inc	$ 1.7250	$ 1.6250	$ 1.5250	$ 1.3950	$ 1.2800	$ 1.2400
Toromont Industries Ltd	$ 0.9200	$ 0.7600	$ 0.7200	$ 0.6800	$ 0.6000	$ 0.5200
Canadian Western Bank	$ 1.0200	$ 0.9400	$ 0.9200	$ 0.8800	$ 0.8000	$ 0.7200
Atco Ltd., Cl.I,	$ 1.5064	$ 1.3100	$ 1.1400	$ 0.9900	$ 0.8600	$ 0.7500

Further to the right you'll see Highest Yield percentages, which could be used to calculate the 10 Average Yields.

idend All-Star List dgrowthinvestingandretirement.com/canad Company	Highest Yield 2018	Highest Yield 2017	Highest Yield 2016	Highest Yield 2015	Highest Yield 2014	Highest Yield 2013
Canadian Utilities	5.48%	4.15%	4.30%	4.00%	3.03%	2.90%
Fortis Inc	4.48%	4.17%	4.29%	4.08%	4.30%	4.20%
Toromont Industries Ltd	2.03%	1.88%	2.64%	2.55%	2.45%	2.46%
Canadian Western Bank	4.19%	4.09%	4.78%	4.18%	2.77%	2.66%
Atco Ltd., CI.I.	4.36%	3.05%	3.44%	2.98%	1.98%	1.89%

We'll use the "DivGth" worksheet to enter these 10-year dividends and the Yields, which will also calculate the 10 Yr. DivGth % and the 10 Yr Ave Yield. I'll enter FTS figures:

FTS	2009	2010	2011	2012	2013	2014	2015	2016	2017	2018	Gth/Yld Ave
Dividend	1.04	1.12	1.16	1.20	1.24	1.28	1.40	1.53	1.63	1.73	65.87%
Ave Yld	4.81%	4.35%	3.98%	3.77%	4.20%	4.30%	4.08%	4.29%	4.17%	4.48%	4.24%

OK, I've provided some different sources to find and enter the dividend data to be entered into the Excel worksheets, which you will then use to decide which stocks should make your "List of stocks to consider".

When you have finished your analysis, you may wish to compare your results to mine.

I eliminated 43 of the TSX 60 at first, but after applying the exception rules, I added 5 back in, resulting in a final tally of 38 cut and 22 quality stocks out of 60 for my: "List of Stocks to Consider".

There is no right or wrong answer on how many you eliminate or keep. I think less is better if you are just starting your income investment journey. I want to keep things simple by sticking with the best dividend growth stocks you can find.

You do not have to buy or even consider buying all the stocks on your list, you are just complying a list of stocks to choose from, when they are reasonably priced (which is discussed later). When it comes to purchasing stocks, it will be much easier to choose from 15 or 20 than 60.

As I mentioned before there will always be exceptions on whether to add a stock or not. Consider each on their unique merits. I'd rather you feel you've selected the best, not the most. I hope you, like me, will be attracted to the "Steady Eddies": the stocks with a long history of sharing their earnings, these stocks increase their payout to shareholders each year. Again, you do not have to buy or consider buying all the stocks on your list. You are just determining potential companies to purchase, so you don't have to look for new stocks or consider stocks which you have not evaluated.

I'll talk more about dividend growth later, but if you find a company that increases their dividend each year, even if it's only by as little as 5%, remember that it is this percentage increase that will build your future wealth. The growth may begin slowly, but the longer you hold the stocks and the more funds you add over time, the faster your income will grow. We are not looking for short-term quick growth, but long-term sustained growth.

Personal Note: The four-rule test is much more important than it may seem at first glance. It almost seems too simple to believe that it actually works, but I can confirm that it really does. Use it every chance you get to analyze any stock or stocks within a fund. I think you'll come to the same conclusion I have, that the four-rule test is an easy and quick way to determine if a company is a quality income (dividend) stock. That's our main focus, finding stocks that will generate the income you seek.

Other items to consider

By performing the four-rule test on the TSX 60 stocks, you might be satisfied with the list generated as is, but there are a few more things you might wish to examine before making your final selections. The following section will concentrate on this next level of analysis:

Check a company's long-term dividend history chart:

To check the "Long-Term Dividend Charts" of companies, go

to The Dividend Channel online: https

For Canadian stocks and funds add .CA after the symbol. We are checking stocks on the TSX 60, and I will use ARX Resources (ARX) as an example. You may not wish to check all the stocks you have eliminated, but you should check a few just to confirm your initial findings.

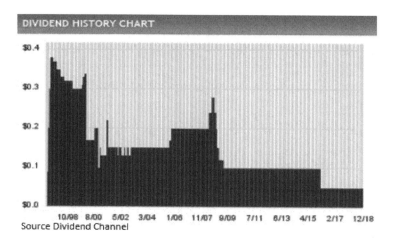

Enter the company symbol "ARX.CA", and review the chart illustrating its dividend history (I have provided a screenshot of the chart above).

If you remember, I easily eliminated ARX using the four-rule test, for cutting their dividend, and after looking at its 20-year dividend chart, it confirms my initial decision. This demonstrates the importance of dividend growth in choosing quality stocks. It also helps to see a company's growth pattern in a visual form, I find these charts very useful as an "at a glance" reference.

Now let's look at BCE.CA's dividend growth history.

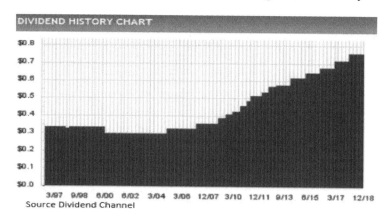

BCE is an example of a four-rule "yes" stock on my list. BCE shows a good dividend growth chart, despite a flat period between 2000 and 2005, and a steady dividend increase after that.

I also want to provide two other examples with AEM and BNS.AEM was first on the TSX 60 list. It cut the dividend but had a dividend growth rate of 128%. But, if you look at its dividend chart, below, you will see how it confirms that it is actually not a quality dividend growth stock:

Symbol	Div Cuts Yes/No	Pd Div 10yrs Yes/No	Raised Div 10yrs Y/N	Div Start	Div End	Div Gth 75% 10Yrs %	Consider Purchase Yes/No Comment	
AEM	Yes	Yes	No	0.18	0.41	127.78%	Cut Div's	
ATD.B	No	Yes	Yes	0.04	0.28	600.00%	Yes, Low Yield, Doubt Gth	

The dividend growth was a result of an extremely low dividend in 2008. However, the chart shows that there has been no real dividend growth since 2007.

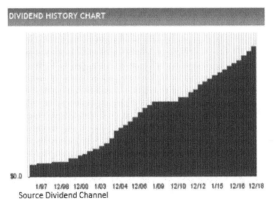

Now look at BNSs chart: Even with only a 58.85% 10-year dividend growth rate, BNS is one I added back to my list of stocks to consider.Just a quick glance at its dividend growth chart explains why!

The BNS long-term dividend chart is almost ideal, a steady and continuous increase over time.

I recommend applying the four-rule test to the stocks before looking at their 20-year dividend chart. As much as I like to recommend reviewing charts, sometimes they can be deceiving, depending upon how they are presented and the number spread used on the chart. The four-rule test and 10-year analysis provides a clearer picture of a company's current status. Use the Dividend Channel charts to view a longer time period, especially for those stocks you might have listed as "exceptions", or when you might want to take another look at a stock that didn't initially make your list.

Review a company's year-to-year dividend yield percentage change:

This is the percentage change of the dividend from one year to the next.

We already performed this calculation as part of the initial four-rule test, but it's so important that I felt it was worth emphasizing here.

It is important to note that the year-to-year change in dividend growth is one of your more important evaluation measurements. We would like to see a consistent growth percentage, one that does not vary too much from year to year.

When there is a sudden or extended drop in the dividend growth rate one should try to find out why. Have earnings dropped? Has the company made some large capital expenditure? Has there been a large loss or lawsuit? The question is, can the decrease be explained, and is it expected to continue or is it a short-term adjustment?

Low Yield, High Dividend growth:

The lower the yield, the less current income, but if the dividend growth is at a higher rate, then over the long-term the dividend growth will likely drive the

CNR

2008	2009	2010	2011	2012	2013	2014	2015	2016	2017	Avg Yield
2.05%	1.76%	1.63%	1.62%	1.66%	1.42%	1.25%	1.62%	1.66%	1.59%	1.63%

price of the stock higher.

With this step I want to demonstrate how a low dividend yield, with a high dividend growth record may be acceptable for long-term investors. Using Morningstar.ca, let's look at Canadian National Railway 's (CNR) current yield. As of this writing, it is 1.58% which is lower than most of the past 10 years and its 10-year average of 1.63%. This indicates that the price has gone up and makes it slightly on the expensive side. But I still consider CNR a good stock to try and buy should the price drop in the future.

Next, let's pay attention to the 10-year average yield of CNR, which is at 1.63% yield and year-to-year percentage change. Look at its dividend growth over the past 10 years which was 258.70%, going from 0.46 in 2008 to 1.65 in 2017 [(1.65-0.46)/0.46 x 100= 258.70%].

I can confirm that this is very good movement, and a reason to consider purchasing a stock with this kind of performance.

CNR

2008	2009	2010	2011	2012	2013	2014	2015	2016	2017	Growth
$ 0.46	$ 0.51	$ 0.54	$ 0.65	$ 0.75	$ 0.86	$ 1.00	$ 1.25	$ 1.50	$ 1.65	258.70%
-	10.87%	5.88%	20.37%	15.38%	14.67%	16.28%	25.00%	20.00%	10.00%	15.38%

Why a good stock's yield is 3% above its average yield:

The higher yield above the 10-year average means the stock is cheaper and offers higher income than normal.

We will now investigate the reason why a stock meeting the basic four-rule test criteria has a dividend yield 3% to 4% above their 10-year average dividend yield. This is not an extremely high yield difference, but it should make one proceed with caution.

Enbridge (ENB) is a good example of this situation. Morningstar shows, as of this writing, that ENB's current yield is 6.40%.

ENB

2008	2009	2010	2011	2012	2013	2014	2015	2016	2017	Avg Yield
3.34%	3.04%	3.02%	2.57%	2.63%	2.71%	2.34%	4.04%	3.75%	4.91%	3.24%

ENB's 10-year average dividend yield is 3.24%

This makes its current yield of 6.31%, higher than the average 10-year yield by 3.17%. Could this be considered a problem?

If you followed the news during this period, you'd know that there was concern about ENB's debt level. Management acknowledged the high debt and promised to sell assets and reduce expenses, which they have. But the market has been weak for all pipelines so the price of ENB has remained low, thus providing a high current yield. In this case, one should look further into the company's debt and the action they've taken, if any, to correct the debt problem. Regardless, one might feel ENB is still a solid stock, its dividend is safe and that this is an opportunity to buy its shares at a discounted price and increase one's income. If you find yourself comfortable with the decisions of management to deal with these financial challenges, then you could proceed to purchase. Remember, the decision is yours.

Consider a company's Payout Ratio:

Payout ratio is the portion of the company's annual earnings being paid out as dividends. To find a business's dividend-**payout ratio** for a given time period, use either the **formula** Dividends paid divided by Net income or Yearly dividends per share divided by Earnings per share. Those formulas are equivalent to each other.

Let's consider a company's Payout Ratio (see Definitions). For most companies 60% to 75% is a reasonable maximum, but utility companies usually go higher, around 80%. Because they often have long-term agreements and regulated prices, they can afford to pay more of their earnings out as dividends. An example of such a company would be Fortis (FTS). Their payout ratio has ranged from 65% to 91%, but the company has still managed to raise its dividend for over 44 years to date. In my opinion, this makes utilities an attractive stock purchase.

Now let's review the payout ratio for BCE. Return to Morningstar.ca and just below the annual dividends, the payout ratio is listed for each year.

	2009-12	2010-12	2011-12	2012-12	2013-12	2014-12	2015-12	2016-12	2017-12	2018-12
Revenue CAD Mil	17,735	18,069	19,497	19,975	20,400	21,042	21,514	21,719	22,719	23,468
Gross Margin %	74.5	72.6	39.1	48.9	48.8	48.5	48.4	49.3	49.5	49.5
Operating Income CAD Mil	3,718	3,896	3,959	4,495	4,709	4,851	5,131	5,280	5,328	5,441
Operating Margin %	21.0	21.6	20.3	22.5	23.1	23.1	23.8	24.3	23.5	23.2
Net Income CAD Mil	1,738	2,277	2,340	2,763	2,106	2,500	2,678	3,031	2,914	2,929
Earnings Per Share CAD	2.11	2.74	2.88	3.17	2.34	2.97	2.98	3.33	3.20	3.10
Dividends CAD	1.58	1.78	2.04	2.22	2.33	2.47	2.60	2.73	2.87	3.02
Payout Ratio % *	74.5	62.6	71.4	65.5	77.4	81.9	84.7	85.3	87.8	97.8
Shares Mil	772	759	771	775	776	795	848	870	894	898
Book Value Per Share * CAD	18.51	19.19	13.57	13.52	14.95	12.68	14.07	14.28	17.00	18.72
Operating Cash Flow CAD Mil	4,875	4,724	4,869	5,552	6,476	6,241	6,274	6,643	7,358	7,384
Cap Spending CAD Mil	-2,854	-2,959	-3,256	-3,515	-3,571	-4,283	-4,161	-3,772	-4,034	-4,027
Free Cash Flow CAD Mil	2,021	1,765	1,613	2,037	2,905	1,958	2,113	2,871	3,324	3,357
Free Cash Flow Per Share * CAD	2.61	2.33	2.14	2.63	2.77	2.83	2.38	3.34	3.71	3.45

Source Morningstar

The payout ratio for BCE has risen over a 10-year period, from 65.2% to 87.8% (paying more of its earnings as dividends). This is high, but the question is whether it's too high. Earnings are shown to have risen from 1.01 to 3.11, up 207%. It appears the dividend has increased faster than earnings and the high payout ratio is a concern. I expect management will slow down the dividend growth to bring the payout ratio down.

Another statistic we can utilize in our analysis is the Free Cash Flow and Free Cash Flow per Share (see Definitions), can be seen lower down on the Key Stats screen. Free cash flow is the cash left over after a company pays for its operating expenses and capital expenditures.

Free Cash Flow CAD Mil	2,899	2,021	1,765	1,613	2,037	2,905	1,958	2,113	2,871	3,324
Free Cash Flow Per Share * CAD	–	2.61	2.33	2.14	2.63	2.77	2.83	2.37	3.34	3.71

Source Morningstar

This shows that BCE has been able to maintain its Free Cash Flow per share high which helps support the dividend increases. So, it's likely that the dividend should be safe but something one might wish to monitor closely over time.

I have not found another source for 10-year payout history, other than Morningstar. In Yahoo under "Statistics" you will see the current payout ratio of the stock listed. Compare the Payout Ratios for stocks in the same sector for a comparison. For example, you might compare the payout ratio of BCE to Telus, or Fortis to Emera.

Avoid high yield stocks:

Stocks with a high dividend yield (in my opinion above 7%) may have difficulty maintaining the dividend (may cut the amount) or not raise the dividend over time.

We will examine how and why to avoid high dividend yield stocks, companies that have yields of 7% and higher with little or no dividend growth.

Here, Corus Entertainment (CJR.B) will make a good example.

Entering the CJR's dividend yields from Morningstar in your Excel spreadsheet, you will see that the last three years,

CJR.B

2008	2009	2010	2011	2012	2013	2014	2015	2016	2017	Avg Yield
-	-	-	-	-	-	-	10.52%	9.05%	9.74%	9.77%

2008	2009	2010	2011	2012	2013	2014	2015	2016	2017	Avg Yield
4.24%	3.02%	2.82%	3.90%	3.88%	3.95%	4.72%	-	-	-	3.79%

Corus' average yield was 9.77%, while the previous 7 years it only averaged 3.79%, a 6% difference.

It was just a matter of time before the dividend was cut, although it wasn't until 2018, but I expect more cuts as the dividend yield has jumped to 21.24%, which is way too high and unsustainable for long.

Avoid cyclical stocks:

Finally, I mentioned avoiding cyclical stocks earlier, now I'd like to explain further. Cyclical stocks are those affected by the ups and downs in the overall economy, such as airline, auto, technology, most energy, retail, consumer and mining stocks. When applying the four-rule test to cyclical stocks on the TSX 60, you will most likely have found they were quickly eliminated, mainly because they normally cut their dividend when they are on a down cycle. Even if you are willing to take chances on stocks that do not fit my criteria, I recommend you avoid stocks that fall into the definition of cyclical.

Once you've put any of these considerations to practical use and seen how they affect any of the stocks on your **"List of Stocks to Consider"**, you may wish to add, remove or just make a note for future reference.

Evaluation tools not considered:

It might be a goodtime to note that we have not looked at many of the other common stock evaluation methods, such as:

- Price to Earnings (P/E), Price to Sales and Price to Cash flow, Return on Equity.
- Estimating the intrinsic value of a stock, the discounted value of the cash that can be taken out of a business during its remaining life.
- Margin metrics, Gross Margin, Operating and Net.
- The Discounted Cash flow, future cash flows are estimated and discounted by using cost of capital to give their present values.

Most of these are used to determine if a stock is expensive, value priced, and/or to project its future earnings potential.

Are they useful? Maybe, but they are more likely to be useful when one is seeking price growth from investments rather than income. This is also not a definitive list, there are as many ways to research and evaluate stocks as there are stock strategies to choose from.

Dividends are real and relevant markers, meaning the company either has the cash to pay the dividend or it does not. Reported earnings, on the other hand, may or may not be actual. I feel comfortable with the handful of steps I have provided and my experience with this method over the years. The point I am trying to make is that my strategy is about simplification, but again I must stress that your comfort level is the priority, feel free to research as many forms of analysis as you wish.

I have narrowed a fairly large selection of companies to a few key dividend growth stocks using yield and dividend growth as our key evaluation measurement. I then applied even more tests for further consideration. It isn't a perfect test, but I do believe that by following the process I've outlined and by adding some common sense for good measure, you should feel comfortable with your results

Your "**List of Stocks to Consider**" should now be complete, at least for the Canadian stocks (unless you wish to apply the four-rules to any other stock or fund). The next steps are:

- Group the stocks into sectors (banks, consumer, pipeline, telecom, utility, etc.).
- When you are ready to buy, choose the stocks, in the same sector, that are currently less expensive, or at least offering a better yield than the others.

- Remember, you do not have to own every stock on your list. You may start with a utility or telecom. Next you may buy a bank or pipeline and so on.
- Be aware that individual stocks and sectors will vary in price at different times.
- Once you've got a portfolio of 10 to 15 stocks in four or five sectors, you might wish to stick with those for a while, adding to them when the price or yield is attractive.
- If the market has a correction, you may be enticed to buy a particular stock which always seemed expensive but is now more reasonable.
- I'd like to reiterate a point I will make often. I'd rather have a lot invested in a few good stocks, rather than the same amount (or more) in a group of mediocre stocks. Less is more.

With your list complete, ignore all other Canadian stocks that did not make your list!

Let's evaluate the XIU ETF:

I mentioned earlier in my book that I do not recommend investing in ETFs (Exchange Traded Funds) for income, and it is only fair that I provide you with some specifics and hope you will come to the same conclusion.

XIU is the ETF which holds the same 60 stocks as the TSX 60. I used the TSX 60 as our source of companies to find qualifying stocks and applied the four-rule test to find our recommended dividend growth stocks. In my own analysis, I was able to eliminate 38 companies or 63.33% of the original 60, and I expect you will come close to the same number with your calculations.

By analyzing the entire XIU ETF, we can see what it would be like to invest in all 60 stocks, rather than the best income providers of the group. Normally we ignore price, but for this comparison it will be meaningful to break this rule.

We will go to Morningstar.ca, find XIU ETF, and then click on "Chart", then "10-years".

You will see that XIU's price was $13.25 in Dec 2008 and a high of $24.68 in Jan. 2018, posting an 87% gain.

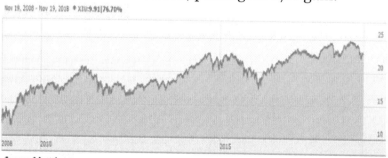

Source Morningstar

However, if you take any of the companies from your own quality stock list, perhaps BCE and review its 10-year chart, you will see that its price goes from $23.06 in Dec. 2008 to $57.52 in Jan. 2018, posting a gain of 150%!

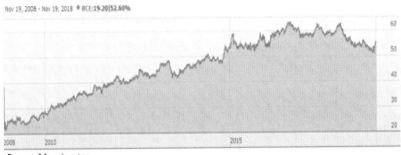

Source Morningstar

You could continue to do the same check with other stocks on your list as I did, and like me, you will likely see that XIU's performance will always be lower than the stocks we separated from the whole. This is a very good example of how lower value stocks will drag down an ETFs overall performance, in my opinion, lessening the attraction and benefit of investing in any ETF.

Personal Note: I checked the 22 stocks on my list and found two that had lower price gains than XIU. Interestingly, I had owned these two and sold them some years back. They still made my List to Consider, but I consolidated to only a few stocks I felt were core holdings.

To even further demonstrate my findings, go to The Dividend Channel website to check XIUs 18-year distributions chart:

https://www.dividendchannel.com/history/?symbol=xiu.ca

Enter "XIU.CA" where it says "Enter Symbol". Scroll down to see the 18-year Distribution chart:

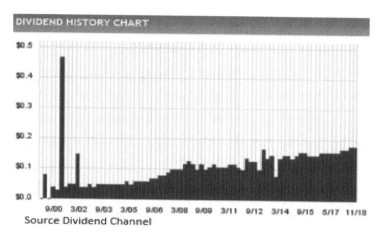
Source Dividend Channel

There does not appear to have been much distribution (income) growth over the past 18 years for this particular ETF.

Compare XIU with BCE's18-year dividend chart:

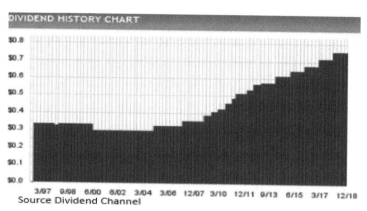
Source Dividend Channel

When you compare the XIU distribution chart to BCE, a "yes" in my (and hopefully your) stock portfolio, XIU comes out the loser. Feel free to check some of the other companies' dividend charts from your "List of Stocks to Consider".

Further down, on the Dividend Channel, you can see on the right 18 years of XIU's quarterly distributions, from 2000 to 2018. I added up the quarterly distributions and entered 10 years, from 2008, on a yearly basis in an Excel spreadsheet.

XIU ETF Distributions

2008	2009	2010	2011	2012	2013	2014	2015	2016	2017	Growth
$ 0.475	$ 0.427	$ 0.446	$ 0.443	$ 0.482	$ 0.529	$ 0.569	$ 0.613	$ 0.454	$ 0.624	31.37%
-	-10.11%	4.45%	-0.67%	8.80%	9.75%	7.56%	7.73%	-25.94%	37.44%	

Notice that the distributions have several negative years and under the "Growth" column you see it listed as 31.37%. This is less than half of our required 75% 10-year DG requirement from our four-rule test. Are you wondering why, or have you already figured out the answer? 60% of XIU's stocks are not quality DG stocks, therefore, besides getting poor price growth there is also little income growth. A double whammy and more than enough reason, in my mind, to avoid this ETF.

I have provided six other well-established Canadian ETFs in Appendix E for your review. Their distribution charts, price charts and the dividend growth percentages are shown to emphasize the points made in my analysis of XIU.

Not many would recommend investing in a new stock (IPO)for income, because without an earnings and performance history these stocks are considered speculative. Yet when a new ETF is rolled out there always seems to be a lot of excitement as they are touted as offering great diversification and low fees. That's the carrot, but where's the distribution and performance history? Perhaps they are not as speculative as an IPO but I feel they are just as uncertain, especially for an income investor.

If I haven't quite been able to convince you why, as an income investor, you should avoid ETFs, here is one more example I hope will do the trick. Vanguard Canada is one of the country's largest ETF providers. They have added five new ETFs, created by combining several of their existing ETFs:

1. The Conservative Income ETF (VCIP) hold 80% bonds and 20% stocks,
2. The Conservative ETF (VCNS) holds 60% bonds and 40% stocks,
3. The Balanced ETF (VBAL) holds 60% stocks and 40% bonds,
4. The Aggressive ETF (VGRO) holds 80% stocks and 20% bonds.
5. The All-Equity ETF (VEQT) is 100% stocks.

On the outside, these "All-in-One" ETFs would seem to offer something for everyone. Touted as total simplicity with low fees, no longer needing to worry about diversification, asset allocation and rebalancing. They will take care of it all, but I am simply not convinced of the benefits of these ETFs. Perhaps an analogy will help illustrate my point:

A man walks into a bar and asks for a glass of the best whiskey in the house, with water. The bartender carefully measures one ounce of his best spirit, then... abruptly pours it into a gallon of water and stirs! He nonchalantly pours out a glass, passes it to the man, and without a hint of irony says, "The first glass is on the house".

All five of the Vanguard funds have a whopping twelve thousand holdings each! Yes, I said 12,000. These funds must hold almost every stock and bond on the planet and trying to identify the best of their holdings might be akin to being able to taste the whiskey in that glass.

Chapter 4

Dividends are a wonderful gauge for management's confidence in forward looking profitability. (Paul Lim, New York Times, May 2, 2009)

What should the dividend yield be when buying?

I have mentioned checking a stock's current yield through the website Morningstar and comparing it to the stock's 10-year average yield to determine if the stock is reasonably priced or expensive. But how do you interpret this information and decide what yield makes a stock worth purchasing?

I feel that a high yield, above 7%and higher, is too high. These stocks will either be speculative (offering a high yield to entice investors), or stocks which may be experiencing financial difficulty (the perception of the stock is negative, driving down the price).

However, there are still a couple of choices to be made involving yields below 7%. Two possible scenarios to consider are the following:

1. A stock with a low dividend yield of 1.5% and less, but with a fairly high dividend growth rate of around 10% to 12% per year, or
2. A stock with an average dividend yield of 2.5% to 5% with an average dividend growth rate of around 5% to 8%.

I recommend that there is a place in one's portfolio for both, but my preference would be to hold a majority of stocks with a starting dividend yield of between 2.5 to 5%.Average-dividend yield stocks offer higher income from the start than low-yield stocks, and likely more sustainable dividend growth over time. This is especially true if the stock has a long history of growing the dividend at a reasonable rate, around 5% to 8%. For example, a stock with an initial dividend yield of 4% which grows its dividend 5% per year would have a yield of 7.92% after 15 years, which I feel is very reasonable. Low initial dividend yields around 0.62% and growth of 15% per year would result in a 4.4% dividend yield after 15 years. Not a great yield after 15 years, but price growth may be higher.

Stocks with a low yield and high dividend growth usually do offer higher capital appreciation (the price of their shares growing), provided they can continue to maintain their high dividend growth rate (usually 10% and above). Two examples are ATD.B and CNR. I'd like to do a comparison of the two.

ATD.B, with a 2018 dividend yield of 0.062%, has only paid a dividend since 2005, but looking at the dividend growth going from 0.04 in 2008 to 0.28 in 2018, that's a **600%** gain.

Here is ATD.B's dividend chart:

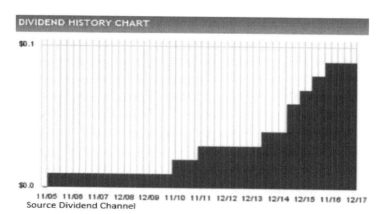

Source Dividend Channel

CNR, with a 2018 dividend yield of 1.58%, has a long and celebrated history which begins in 1995 when they were once a government-owned corporation.

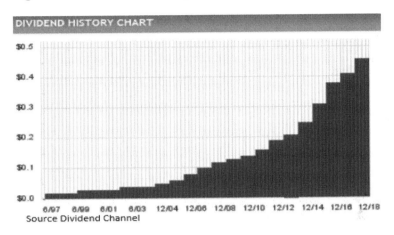

DIVIDEND HISTORY CHART

Source Dividend Channel

Here's the Year to Year dividend percentage growth of each:

		2008	2009	2010	2011	2012	2013	2014	2015	2016	2017	Div Gth
ATD-B	Dividend	0.04	0.05	0.05	0.09	0.10	0.11	0.15	0.19	0.25	0.28	600.00%
	Yr by Yr		25.0%	0.0%	80.0%	11.1%	10.0%	36.4%	26.7%	31.6%	12.0%	
CNR	Dividend	0.51	0.54	0.65	0.75	0.86	1.00	1.25	1.50	1.65	1.82	256.86%
	Yr by Yr		5.9%	20.4%	15.4%	14.7%	16.3%	25.0%	20.0%	10.0%	10.3%	

ATD.B did have a higher growth rate in the past 10 years, but I believe CNR shows a more consistent growth over the long-term, but which would you choose?

We can't predict the future growth rate of each stock, but we do have support for our assumptions every time they pay and raise their dividend. If the low-yield, high-growth company can maintain its high growth rate, then the stock will offer a higher total return than the average-yield stocks in the long run.

Back to the question of what the starting yield should be. I don't recommend a particular starting yield, rather I suggest that when you are looking to buy a stock, based on your research, try to find stocks with a high yield in the sector of your choice. I do hesitate to buy, or recommend you buy, a stock with a yield less than 1%.

How many stocks should you hold?

Seek quality individual stocks in a concentrated portfolio with low turnover (hold) and focus on the valuable far-flung future cash flow. (Tom Connolly, The Connolly Report)

How many stocks to hold in your portfolio(s) is a personal choice, there is no magic number. Some suggest 30, 50 or even 100 or more. The higher numbers are suggested in order that you hold sufficient stocks to be appropriately diversified (holding stocks in different sectors). Do not let others convince you to hold a large number of stocks across multiple sectors just to diversify. Again, you need to determine what your investment goals are, then build a portfolio accordingly.

However, if you are considering an income portfolio, I suggest starting with a lower number and then add only when you find a stock which meets your buy criteria. Don't just add stocks for diversification's sake, instead select stocks which will provide you with the income growth you are seeking. I've seen portfolios of 40 to 50 stocks and, in some cases, only a few dollars invested in each. That seems like a shotgun approach, especially when you are just starting out. Instead, I want you to identify those good "Steady Eddies" and buy as many shares as you can at a reasonable price. Kick-start your income growth-machine as quickly as possible.

You may still not be convinced that less is the way to go. Perhaps the following example will help persuade you.

One day I read a very interesting headline;

"RBC executives may sell 30,000 shares." - IE Investment Executive, July 6, 2005

Wow, I thought, how many shares do these RBC executives own? Probably more than most individual investors could ever accumulate. And why would they think of selling?

With this example, I want to show you the advantage of holding just one good DG stock, if the circumstances are to your advantage. In 2005, the Royal Bank dividend was $1.175 per share. If you only owned the Royal Bank stock, and held 30,000 shares in 2005, your annual income (dividends) would have been $35,250. Jump ahead to 2018 and you would now receive $114,000 per year of income (without reinvesting the dividends which would have increased the income considerably), a 223% increase in 14 years and an average of 9.64%/year.

Better yet, look at the chart at left, and you will see that the income you would have received over the 14 years is **$1 Million!**

Check your four-rule test results for Royal Bank and couple that with their long history of paying and growing their dividend, it should lead you to the conclusion that it is likely that Royal Bank will continue as a good DG stock.

Year	Shares	Div	Div Inc	Inc %
2005	30,000	1.18	$35,400	
2006	30,000	1.44	$43,200	22.03%
2007	30,000	1.82	$54,600	26.39%
2008	30,000	2.00	$60,000	9.89%
2009	30,000	2.00	$60,000	0.00%
2010	30,000	2.00	$60,000	0.00%
2011	30,000	2.08	$62,400	4.00%
2012	30,000	2.28	$68,400	9.62%
2013	30,000	2.53	$75,900	10.96%
2014	30,000	2.76	$82,800	9.09%
2015	30,000	3.04	$91,200	10.14%
2016	30,000	3.20	$96,000	5.26%
2017	30,000	3.48	$104,400	8.75%
2018	30,000	3.80	$114,000	9.20%
14 Years of Income			$1,008,300	9.64%

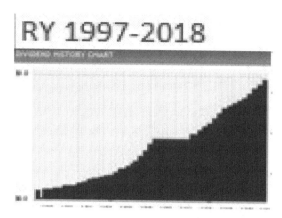

Its dividend is most likely safe and will continue to grow as it has in the past. So, if you're fortunate enough to have 30,000 shares of a solid DG stock like Royal Bank, would you be concerned that you are not diversified? You would do better to hold on to it and take advantage of the growing income, rather than the one-time payoff of selling, or sell some of the shares to buy others just to diversify.

Owning 30,000 shares of any stock is unrealistic for the average person, but what if you owned 300 shares in 2005? Let's look at the income you would have received over 14 years.

The chart on the left shows how much income you'd receive if the dividend stayed fixed at the 2005 rate. The right side is with the actual dividends paid (no dividend increases for 3 years, 2008-2010). Dividends are reinvested in both cases,

Royal Bank Div Fixed				Royal Bank Actual Div's			
Year	Shares	Div Rec	Inc Gth %	Year	Shares	Div Rec	Inc Gth %
2004	300.00			2004	300.00		
2005	315.92	$637.04		2005	316.78	$674.53	
2006	651.58	$667.45	4.77%	2006	657.44	$902.15	33.74%
2007	664.76	$682.77	2.30%	2007	679.53	$1,144.94	26.91%
2008	680.04	$696.86	2.06%	2008	709.81	$1,379.96	20.53%
2009	696.08	$714.56	2.54%	2009	742.25	$1,447.98	4.93%
2010	709.43	$729.01	2.02%	2010	769.81	$1,504.64	3.91%
2011	723.98	$742.99	1.92%	2011	801.11	$1,592.17	5.82%
2012	737.72	$758.38	2.07%	2012	833.79	$1,805.98	13.43%
2013	749.62	$772.02	1.80%	2013	865.84	$2,081.52	15.26%
2014	759.69	$783.69	1.51%	2014	896.91	$2,423.01	16.41%
2015	770.03	$794.02	1.32%	2015	932.96	$2,766.57	14.18%
2016	780.16	$805.04	1.39%	2016	971.09	$3,033.97	9.67%
2017	788.60	$814.68	1.20%	2017	1005.79	$3,345.88	10.28%
2018	796.85	$823.31	1.06%	2018	1043.53	$3,772.53	12.75%
Total Div Rec'd		$9,784.77	2.00%	Total Div Rec'd		$27,201.31	14.45%
				Income Difference		178.00%	

o I feel confident stating that investing in a quality dividend growth stock is a much more sound and profitable strategy than fixed income/low growth GICs, bonds and ETFs.

I want to leave you with the idea that instead of worrying about how many stocks to own, concentrate on owning a smaller number of carefully selected stock picks. Stick to your own carefully curated list and avoid stocks that you haven't researched yourself, and avoid buying a bundle of stocks which will dilute your income. I am also not assigning a minimum number of stocks to hold, but rather recommend that you take advantage of buying opportunities of quality dividend growth (DG) stocks when the price drops. And, if you refer to the example of the Royal Bank from above, the more you have invested in fewer numbers of high performing dividend growth stocks, the better your income return will be. Remember, quality over quantity.

This is the foundation of my investing strategy and how I suggest you build an income-generating machine.

Personal Note: My wife and I at one time held between 35 and 40 stocks in all our accounts, but gradually eliminated most and now hold only 12 stocks in two RRIF, two TFSA, a joint account and our DRIPs. We eliminated much of our portfolio because I continually reassessed our holdings and found some were not quality companies anymore, did not perform as well as we expected or had bought some stocks only for their higher yield. In hind sight we now know we would have been much better off with the concentrated portfolio right from the start. I hope to help you avoid my earlier missteps and start growing your income as soon as possible!

> Those who cannot remember the past are condemned to repeat it. (George Santayana)

When does price matter?

> [I]f you are a saver and a buyer of shares—as most investors are and will continue to be for many years—your real long-term interest is, curiously, to have stock prices go down quite a lot and stay there so you can accumulate more shares at lower prices and therefore receive more dividends with the savings you invest. (Charles Ellis, Winning the Loser's Game)

> For the stock you are considering to purchase, what we want is one with a good initial yield with a sustainable dividend growth. (Tom Connolly, *The Connolly Report*)

If you are investing small amounts of money, the price you pay for a stock should not be a concern (within reason). I want you to invest often and try to build up your holdings as quickly as possible. Let Dollar-Cost Averaging, which is buying more shares when the price is low and less when the price is high, even out the average cost of your investment.

For those investing larger amounts, try to buy when the price is low and/or your yield higher (a lower price means you will be buying more shares, and the higher yield means that you will be receiving more income). This does not mean waiting for the next market correction or trying to time the market, but, seeking reasonably priced stocks and knowing you are not paying a high price.

Here are a few simple methods to determine if the stock you wish to buy is value-priced (the price is low) and offers a good initial yield.

1. Compare the stocks' current yield (current annual dividend divided by the current price) against its 10-year average yield: Again, I will use BCE to assist with our analysis. The 10-year average yield is shown on your worksheet when you completed your

BCE	11-Dec-09	13-Dec-10	13-Dec-11	12-Dec-12	12-Dec-13	11-Dec-14	11-Dec-15	13-Dec-16	14-Dec-17	13-Dec-18	10 Yr Gth%
Dividend	1.58	1.79	2.05	2.22	2.33	2.47	2.60	2.73	2.87	3.02	91.14%
Div Gth Yr		13.04%	14.61%	8.55%	4.95%	6.00%	5.18%	5.08%	5.12%	5.15%	
Price	27.47	36.37	40.88	44.31	46.76	56.36	56.43	58.66	57.52	57.13	10yr Ave Yld
Yield %	5.75%	4.91%	5.01%	5.01%	4.99%	4.39%	4.61%	4.66%	4.99%	5.29%	4.96%
Current Yld	5.29%										

   initial analysis of BCE:

The 10-year average yield is listed at the bottom right of the worksheet, shown as 4.95% above.

You will see that BCE's current yield is 5.29% showing that BCE is offering a higher yield than its average, which is good.

2. Another method is to compare the current price of the stock to the 52-week low price. *The Globe and Mail* provides a way to view daily updates of stock prices. Just go to their website, https://www.theglobeandmail.com/investing/markets/portfolio/#/,

	A	B	C	D	E	F	G	H	I
1			As of October 26, 2018					Percentage	Percentage
2			Latest			52 Weeks		Drop to	from High
3	Company	Symbol	Price	High	Low	High	Low	Low Price	to Low $
4	BCE Inc.	BCE-T	51.56	52.71	51.32	62.90	50.72	1.66%	24.01%
5	Bank of Montreal	BMO-T	98.86	99.48	97.92	109.00	93.60	5.62%	16.45%
6	Bank of Nova Scotia	BNS-T	69.99	70.14	69.02	85.50	69.01	1.42%	23.90%

and set up a portfolio (you should be using the stocks you have chosen using the four-rule test). Concentrate on the 52-week high and the low prices.

Compare the current price of the stock you are considering buying to its 52-week high and low price. If the current price is closer to the high price than the stock is probably too expensive, or at least has been rising over the 52-week period. If the price is closer to the lower price, than likely the price has dropped making it a better stock to consider purchasing. Did you notice that BCE on Oct. 26, 2018 was $51.56, much closer to the 52-week low of $50.72 than the high of $62.90? This makes the current price on the low side, which matches our assessment that the current yield of 5.29% is higher than normal.

3. For the third method, I recommend you set up an Excel worksheet to project what the dividend yield would be if the current price drops 3%, 5%, 8%, etc.

Price Oct 15\18	Current Div	Current Yield	Ave 10 yr Yield	3% Price Drop	Yield	5% Price Drop	Yield	8% Price Drop	Yield	10% Price Drop	Yield
$51.56	$3.02	5.86%	4.89%	$50.01	6.04%	$48.98	6.17%	$47.44	6.37%	$46.40	6.51%
$40.96	$2.68	6.55%	3.33%	$39.73	7.60%	$38.91	7.76%	$37.68	8.01%	$36.86	8.19%

If the stock price drops you can quickly see what yield you would receive, the chart I have provided shows the yield rises as the price decreases. The higher the yield the more income you will receive for each dollar invested. That's a good thing!

87

4. The fourth method uses the Adjusted Cost Base (ACB) or the average cost of your stocks (if you already own stocks you will be familiar with this term). You can compare the current price of any stock you are considering buying to the ACB of the same stock you own. If the current price is close or lower than the ACB it may be a good time to buy.

5. Lastly, when you place your order with an online broker you can enter a "limit" price. This is the price you want to pay for the stock. The broker will not buy until the price reaches the price you set. You could intentionally enter a low price, of around 10% of the current price, leave the bid open for a month or so and wait to see if the order gets filled.

If we continue reviewing BCE, you will see that during the next 30 days BCE never hit the low price of $50.72 and, by the end of November 2018, the price was $56.95 with a yield of 5.30%. There is no way to determine which way the market will go, so if you feel a stock is offering a good yield, as I feel BCE was at 5.29%, you could buy at least some shares.

If a stock's yield is lower than its average (which indicates that the stock is expensive), don't feel you have to jump in immediately to buy. Stock prices can vary as much as 50%, though that's not the norm, over a 52-week period. If you don't get a stock at the price you want, don't worry as it's likely the price may drop later on. Be patient, or you can always keep researching for a more value-priced stock from your quality stock list.

We are not trying to buy at the lowest price possible (trying to time your purchases), but attempting to pay a reasonable price and ensure the purchases will contribute to our growing income. If you decided on a buy price, don't get upset if the price drops after you have bought. Continue to monitor the price and buy again when you have funds.

The exception is when there is a major correction in the stock market. We can't predict when or what might cause a correction, how low the market will drop or how long the market will stay down. There are many short-term market corrections which may only last a day or two, but a major correction, one which would cause a recession, can easily last months or even a year. During these major crises you will find the market low will be tested several times, so don't feel you need to jump in immediately. What you should do is revise your Yield projections for each stock on your list and you might look to buy a stock which you always considered expense. It's during these major market corrections you will have the opportunity of boosting your income and your total yield on your investments (discussed later).

Reinvested Dividends:

> Without dividend reinvestment, annual returns from stocks would be about as exciting as watching a silent movie. (Bill Staton, *America's Finest Companies Investment Plan,* 1989)

With dividend paying companies you have the choice of taking the money (leaving it in your broker account) or using the cash dividend to buy more shares. Every time you use your dividends to buy more shares you increase your next dividend payment. If you reinvest again you buy even more shares and the cycle repeats itself. Dividend reinvestment is one of the most important parts of my income investment strategy. Most brokers only allow dividends received to buy whole shares, not fractions of shares. If you receive a $65.00 cash dividend and the current price of that share is $57.50, $7.50 remains in the account. That's ok, if one is adding funds regularly to their account, the unused cash can be added to their next purchase.

Many investors prefer to let the dividends accumulate in their account and combine them with new funds for their next purchase. Personally, I find this highly inefficient. What if you don't make the next purchase immediately or next month or even next quarter? Why not take advantage of commission-free reinvestment, even if only to ensure the regular accumulation of shares?

The three keys to enhanced compounding are: buying quality dividend growth stocks, buying shares when they are value-priced and reinvesting the dividends.

That's what I mean by compounding, and I cannot emphasize enough its value as an income investment tool.

This subscribes to my philosophy of "hands-off" investing, by utilizing automatic reinvesting it takes a lot of work off your shoulders. You are in the process of constantly acquiring shares, and those new shares will collect dividends and your dividends will become larger, and the cycle repeats.
*Reinvesting dividends along with dividend growth is exactly what I mean by an ever-growing income!

For those just beginning, who invest only periodically, or are retired and no longer adding funds, you should try to accumulate fractions of shares, rather than only full shares with Full Dividend Reinvestment. ~~ShareOwners Investment Inc. is the only Canadian broker which offers Full Dividend Reinvestment. However, one of the draw backs with ShareOwners is that you cannot place "limit" orders (specifying the price you wish to buy a stock for). This is not necessarily a negative, but if you are price-driven, you might have to compromise on this point. To me, the constant accumulation of shares beats price-watching.~~

To prove my point, I'd like you to look back to the example of my grandson (covered in Chapter 1). If I exclude the fractions of shares, he was able to purchase, he would have only bought 60 full shares over the 11-year period. But he actually bought 80.9445 shares by being able to buy fractions of shares with his dividends. He received almost 21 additional shares or 33.33% more by simply utilizing dividend reinvestment.

That's a lot of extra shares that might not have been bought otherwise, a lot more income and very nice compounding, don't you agree?

How, where and what to invest:

> Think of stocks not only as providing a stream of income but actually as streams of income. You exchange your money for future cash flow. As the income grows with dividend increases, your original capital can grow too. An annuity, but better. (Josh Peters, founding editor of *Morningstar DividendInvestor*)

Dividend Reinvestment Plan (DRIP):

I don't want you to confuse Reinvesting Dividends, discussed in the previous section, with a Dividend Reinvestment Plan (DRIP). A DRIP is an investment plan offered directly by companies and does not require one to open a brokerage account to buy shares or reinvest the dividends. DRIPs are ideally suited for those with limited funds to invest, perhaps less than $100 per month, or if you are investing for a minor. In addition to a DRIP, the company must also offer Share Purchase Plans (SPP), which allows one to buy additional shares from the company. Not all DRIP companies offer SPP. The advantages of investing by DRIPs and SPP are that one can invest small amounts commission free and the reinvested dividends purchase fractions of shares. (I discuss DRIPs and SPPs in more detail in Chapter 5.)

Tax-Free Savings Accounts (TFSA):

Every investor, 18 years and older, should take advantage of this tax-free account. Considering all gains within the TFSA and withdrawals are tax-free, it's a huge opportunity to grow your portfolio. Another advantage is that previous years of under-contributions can be combined with any future contributions. I would suggest one try to invest the available maximum in their TFSA before investing in other accounts,

DRIP is an exception if you're only investing small amounts. Taxes should not be a concern with a DRIP, if one's total current taxable income is low. I find that three to five DG stocks are all one needs in a TFSA. On a happy note, the 2019 maximum TFSA contribution has now been raised from $5,500 to $6,000 a year.

You should also be aware that there are some restrictions with the TFSA, such as not being able to withdraw funds and then re-contribute the same amount in the same year. You can easily find more details online.

Registered Education Savings Plan (RESP):

No one should pass up free money, especially if you have children and post-secondary education is in their future. The federal government matches 20% of the first $2,500 contributed annually to a RESP, to a maximum of $500 per beneficiary per year. The lifetime maximum per beneficiary is $7,200, up to age 18. I highly recommend that if you have the funds to spare, you load up all your RESP accounts with one or more DG stocks. The only catch might be if the RESP is started when the kids are older, as the timeframe may become too short to benefit from stocks.

Registered Retirement Savings Plan (RRSP):

If you have the funds, after maxing out your TFSA, and after investing in RESPs for your children, then you could also try to max out your RRSP(s). The nice part of RRSP contributions is that they reduce your current year's taxes. RRSPs can be considered a good investment choice, made even better when they are loaded with dividend growth stocks. I will always recommend that dividend growth stocks be the only investment product you load into any of your plans. It is worth adding here that it has also been suggested that any tax dollars saved be invested, but to be honest I doubt many do it. I ascribe to the belief that any opportunity to invest in your future should be taken, the more often you do it, the easier it becomes.

US Dividend Growth Stocks:

At this time, I would like to address investment in US dividend growth stocks. If you wish to hold US dividend growth stocks, they should be held in your RRSP to avoid the 15% tax on the dividends.

To determine which US DG stocks to invest in you could refer to the NOBL ETF which contains 57 of the US Dividend Aristocrats. These are US stocks that have raised their dividend for at least 25 years (see Appendix C), a great starting point.

You could buy the NOBL ETF, but be aware that, like the TSX 60, not all the stocks listed are equal. To illustrate my point, I applied the four-rule test to the entire roster of NOBL stocks and eliminated28but added back two as exceptions, therefore eliminating 26 companies or 47.37% of the original 57, and I expect you will come close to the same number with your calculations.

The NOBL ETF has only been in existence since 2013 and

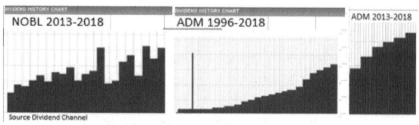

you can see its dividend history chart below. The two on the right (one 2013-2018) is Archer Daniels Midland Co., or ADM, which passed my four-rule test. ADM's chart goes back to 1996. I think it is obvious which looks like a better dividend payer/growth performer.

Here are two other stocks (below) from NOBL. How do these two charts compare to ADM and would you consider them good DG stocks, even though they have increased their dividend for 25 years?

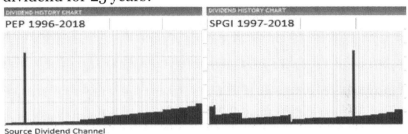

Source Dividend Channel

This is another example of why I always emphasize research and analyzing individual stock performance and how lower quality stocks will drag down the performance of ETFs. You would not catch differences like this if you simply purchased the entire ETF.

The US has many good DG stocks to choose from, so you could tighten your guidelines even more and still have a healthy amount that will qualify. You could, for example, raise the Dividend Growth percentage to 95% from 75% over 10 years, but also feel free to allow for exceptions as well. I would especially watch the 10-year "year-to-year" dividend percentage changes. Ideally, we would like to see a consistent dividend growth, we are looking for the "Steady Eddies", remember? At the end of the day, if you find five to ten US DG stocks you are comfortable with that should be all you need.

Non-registered accounts:

Finally, if you can feel free to invest in low-yield, high-growth DG stocks through non-registered accounts. It's important to remember that the dividends in the non-registered accounts are taxed, though at a lower rate than regular income, so try and keep the dividend income low and go for price growth. The need for a non-registered account might arise if you have maxed out all other accounts. If you originally opened a DRIP, I would not close that account, but leave it, or even continue to add to it as there are no fees to do so. If the DRIP account gets too large, transfer shares to your TFSA to save on taxes.

Other Investments:

Other than Dividend Growth stocks, fixed income, ETFs and mutual funds, I will take this opportunity to mention some other popular investments, such as:

REIT's:

> Real Estate Investment Trusts. These usually offer higher initial yields, but not always. They payout most of the company's earnings, thereby avoiding taxes, which are passed on to the people who buy the shares.

> Most of their earnings are paid out, so there is limited earnings growth, distribution (dividend) increases and price growth, if any. Here are five REIT examples showing their yearly distributions, 10-year dividend percentage growth rate and price charts (for 3).

H & R REIT 6.58% Yield, HR.UN, 10-yr distributions:

2008	2009	2010	2011	2012	2013	2014	2015	2016	2017	Div Gth
1.44	0.72	0.79	0.97	1.18	1.35	1.35	1.35	1.35	1.38	-4.17%

Riocan REIT 5.74% Yield, REI.UN, 10-yr distributions:

2008	2009	2010	2011	2012	2013	2014	2015	2016	2017	Div Gth
1.36	1.38	1.38	1.38	1.38	1.41	1.41	1.41	1.41	1.41	3.68%

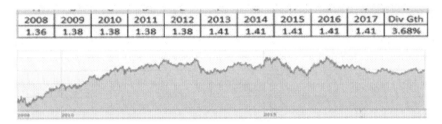

Artis REIT 10.68% Yield, AX.UN, 10-yr distributions:

2008	2009	2010	2011	2012	2013	2014	2015	2016	2017	Ave Yld
1.07	1.08	1.08	1.08	1.08	1.08	1.08	1.08	1.08	1.08	0.93%

CUF.UN

2018	2017	2016	2015	2014	2013	2012	2011	2010	2009	2008	Div Gth
0.790	1.336	1.475	1.474	1.455	1.440	1.440	1.440	1.440	1.440	1.417	-44.25%

BEI.UN

2018	2017	2016	2015	2014	2013	2012	2011	2010	2009	2008	Div Gth
0.996	2.256	2.238	3.040	3.435	1.975	1.895	1.800	2.300	1.800	1.800	-44.67%

Apply our four-rule test to any REIT (use Dividend Channel) you are considering adding to your portfolio. Don't get excited by their higher yields, as there is little, if any, dividend and price growth, as shown in the three charts provided. Most REITs, in my opinion, fall into the high-yield, low (NO) growth investments. However, should you still wish to own some, buy them in the registered accounts to avoid paying tax.

British ADRs:

	2008	2009	2010	2011	2012	2013	2014	2015	2016	2017	2018	Div Gth
AZN	0.95	1.04	1.21	1.35	1.43	1.40	1.40	1.40	1.40	1.40	1.40	47.37%
ABB	0.45	0.43	0.47	0.67	0.70	0.72	0.77	0.77	0.75	0.76		68.89%
BBL	1.64	1.66	1.82	2.20	2.28	2.36	2.48	1.56	1.08	1.96		19.51%
BCS	0.00	0.00	0.00	0.00	0.00	0.00	0.00	0.00	0.00	0.00		0.00%
BP	3.30	3.36	0.84	1.68	1.98	2.19	2.34	2.40	2.40	2.40		-27.27%
BT	0.82	0.15	0.34	0.36	0.42	0.48	0.57	0.64	0.74	0.76		-7.32%
BTI	0.66	0.92	1.06	1.19	1.33	1.41	1.45	1.52	1.56	2.19		231.82%
CAJ	104.46	111.26	126.20	142.34	198.38	132.22	140.81	157.32	155.10	165.73		58.65%
CX	6.40	0.00	0.00	0.00	0.00	0.00	0.00	0.00	0.00	0.00		-100.00%
DEO	1.39	1.49	1.56	1.63	1.82	2.00	2.16	2.30	2.37	2.60		87.05%
GSK	1.13	1.20	1.29	1.35	1.47	1.56	1.60	1.57	1.55	1.61		42.48%
HMC	66.18	46.54	65.09	70.18	73.31	82.02	85.14	90.81	67.10	101.17		52.87%
HSBC	4.65	1.70	1.70	1.95	2.05	2.40	2.45	2.50	2.55	2.55		-45.16%
IHG	0.60	0.60	0.61	0.72	0.84	0.89	0.92	1.00	1.03	0.98		63.33%
INFY	0.04	0.06	0.07	0.09	0.08	0.10	0.15	0.19	0.19	0.22		450.00%
LYG	1.34	0.00	0.00	0.00	0.00	0.00	0.00	0.06	0.09	0.13		-90.30%
NGG	1.80	1.94	2.06	2.02	2.20	2.20	2.29	2.38	2.35	2.24		24.44%
NOK	0.50	0.41	0.31	0.39	0.19	0.00	0.11	0.14	0.26	0.17		-66.00%
NVO	0.64	0.88	1.09	1.92	2.80	3.61	4.51	5.04	9.33	7.58		1084.38%
NVS	1.54	1.71	1.95	2.36	2.48	2.53	2.72	2.67	2.72	2.72		76.62%
PKX	2230.45	2061.80	2427.77	2532.33	1950.57	2018.81	1997.03	1999.68	2077.31	2022.20		-9.34%
PNR	0.68	0.72	0.76	0.80	0.88	0.96	1.10	1.28	1.34	1.38		102.94%
RBS	11.15	0.00	0.00	0.00	0.00	0.00	0.00	0.00	0.00	0.00		-100.00%
RDS-B	3.12	3.32	3.36	3.42	3.56	3.72	3.76	3.76	3.76	3.76		20.51%
RIO	1.52	0.68	0.88	1.16	1.64	1.76	2.03	2.20	1.51	2.36		55.26%
SNE	35.40	25.47	31.89	27.56	26.60	24.93	0.00	19.82	19.10	27.17		-23.25%
SNN	0.25	0.27	0.29	0.32	0.41	0.52	0.87	0.60	0.63	0.61		144.00%
TSM	11.96	11.86	12.03	14.94	14.75	15.18	14.98	0.00	30.38	35.23		194.57%
UL	0.69	0.70	0.86	0.89	0.96	1.04	1.12	1.19	1.26	1.39		101.45%
VOD	1.69	1.63	1.92	2.77	2.23	2.29	1.34	1.56	1.39	1.48		-12.43%

These are British stocks which trade on the US stock market and pay their dividends in US currency. The attraction is that you can hold these stocks in a TFSA and pay no tax on the dividends and you get the benefit of receiving US dollars. I still insist on applying our four-rule test to any fund and did so to a group of 30recommended British ADR stocks. The chart above shows the annual dividends and 10-year dividend growth rate of the thirty stocks. I disqualified 23 of the total30just using my 4-rule test alone. Here's the long-term dividend charts of the seven that met the four-rule test. How many would you keep? One or possibly two?

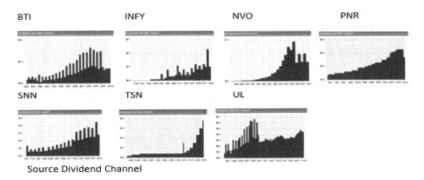

Source Dividend Channel

Also, many of the ADR stocks pay their dividend semi-annually, not quarterly, slowing the compounding.

It is always riskier to invest in foreign companies as it is harder to evaluate performance and gather information on the companies. I prefer companies I can confidently quantify.

I suggest sticking with companies you are familiar with, concentrating on US stocks many of which have extensive foreign investments. Hold US stocks in your RRSP and Canadian stocks in your TFSA. If you applied the four-rule test to the NOBL holdings you will have found many had much higher 10-year dividend growth rates than these ADRs.

Gold:

Gold is usually considered a hedge against rapid inflation; however, it pays no interest or dividends. If you wish to own gold, buy the gold coins from BNS and consider it part of your savings or emergency funds. Do not consider gold as being part of your income investment.

When to sell your stocks?

Like Warren Buffett, a very high profile and respected figure in the financial community, I believe **"*our favorite holding period is forever*"**. However, there are times when you should consider selling some or all of a company's shares:

- If you need the money.
- If the company cuts their dividend.
- If the company does not raise its dividend and you cannot justify holding the stock (it appears they will not raise it again soon),
- If you wish to get rid of stocks which have not performed as expected.
- If a major change effects the company (like a takeover), and you are more comfortable selling than waiting to see if the change is negative or positive.

I hope that you can see that you need to continue to hold your current roster of stocks to the same scrutiny that you applied when you first picked them. You should be monitoring the dividend payments, their increases and especially dividend growth rates of all stocks you own. Don't panic if there is negative news regarding one of your holdings, certainly monitor the news but as long as the monthly or quarterly dividends continue apace, and increase, there should be no reason to sell any of your stocks. The more information we have the better, but remember, we are not price-watching so we should not stress about the volatility of the market.

There is no denying that there are always investors that are looking for a better opportunity and cannot help but get caught up in "the next best thing". I wish them well in their pursuits, but personally, I'd rather keep holding on to my solid Dividend Growth performers, and sit back, relaxed, while my income continues to grow!

Personal note: When I was applying the four-rules to the TSX 60 stocks in preparation for this book, one of my own stocks did not make the list. I did not immediately move to get rid of this stock, rather I checked to ensure it continued to provide the income I expect, and it does. The purpose of the four-rule test is to compile a list of stocks to consider purchasing, it does not necessarily suggest shedding stocks the minute there is a questionable performance issue. This point is to demonstrate that regular assessment is key and provides an ease of mind that your money is always working towards the goals you have set.

Monitoring your portfolio:

> People who can manage their time can also manage their money. After all, managing minutes and managing money is the same exact principle. (Ann Marie Sabath, founder of Ease Inc.)

How should the income investor monitor their portfolio? Well, you will want to avoid a **"Stop-Loss System".** Stop-losses are where one would set a sell price to minimize capital losses should the price of a stock drop. This may be a viable method for those investing for growth or buying and selling shares, but not for dividend growth investors.

For income investors, dividends are what we watch. Most quality dividend growth companies have a regular payment routine. For each quarter the board of directors announces the dividend to be paid the next quarter. However, those that raise their dividend usually do it the same quarter each year. Most Canadian banks raise their dividend twice a year.

Knowing when companies pay and raise their dividend is the key. As long as they meet these pay dates and raise their dividend as expected, you can be assured that the company is in good shape. You don't need to scour the financial statements or listen to the expert opinions. The dividends should be so regular and consistent that you could set your calendar by their confirmation. **Making it easy to monitor an income portfolio:**

As mentioned before, keeping track of the dividend growth percentage from one year to the next year is one of the most important aspects of monitoring your holdings.

The next section covers how to record your investment transactions. One of the more unrecognized advantages of monitoring your portfolio is the thrill of seeing your income grow. Every time your dividend payment is deposited in your accounts, you record it in your worksheets. I have never tired of reviewing my records and I have never lost the pleasure of having my investing decisions confirmed quarter after quarter. I hope you will enjoy this part of the process as much as I have!

Recording your investments:

I'm not referring to tracking the price of your holdings or how much your investments are worth. You can, if you wish, but what you really want to monitor is your income and the income growth.

In order to really appreciate income investing you must track the income your stocks are producing. It's not going to be sudden jumps upward, but a slow and gradual increase over time.

I use an accounting program because I was an accountant and I like to account for the pennies. Excel provides the details and I'll present you with a quick sketch of the reports I've set up and how they work.

```
SHAREOWNER STOCKS:
HENRY'S\TFSA SHAREOWNER CASH
HENRY'S\TFSA SHAREOWNER STKS
  SUB-TOTAL HM TFSA

HENRY RRIF SHAREOWNER CASH
HM STOCKS VALUE
  SUB-TOTAL HM STOCKS

RAE'S RRIF SHAREOWNER CASH
RAE'S RRSP SHAREHOLDER STOCKS
  SUB-TOTAL RM RRSP

JOINT SHAREOWNER CASH
JOINT STOCKS VALUE

  TOTAL JOINT STOCKS

RAE'S\TFSA SHAREOWNER CASH
RAE'S\TFSA SHAREOWNER STKS
  SUB-TOTAL RM TFSA
```

I also use an accounting program, like Quickbooks, where I've set up accounts for each account (RRIFs, TFSAs & Non-Registered), examples are at the left:

All entries are made in the cash accounts, which record deposits, purchases, reinvestments and fees. **The cash account should always balance with the broker cash balance in your accounts.**

In the cash account, most transactions including commissions are coded to the matching stock account (TFSA cash entries are coded to TFSA stocks, and so on). The only transactions coded elsewhere are the account fees that are not related to stock purchases/sales. The sub-total accounts are my total investment in each category. I then use an Excel worksheet with several sub-worksheets where I re-enter the same transactions, but it provides the specific details on each stock and includes many more reports to record and track the income and summarize my holdings.

If you don't have or use an accounting program, then you would want an "Activity" worksheet in Excel. You would record each transaction in the various accounts you hold with the broker. This is how you will verify the cash balance in Excel with the cash balance in the broker's accounts. One always needs a cross-check when working with Excel to

	Transaction Activity Report				
Date	Activity	Shares	Price	Amount	Balance
1-Jun-18	Deposit Funds			50.00	3,000.00
27-Jun-18	Bought	59.0121	42.1956	-2,500.00	500.00
28-Jun-18	Div			47.27	547.27
10-Jul-18	Bought	1.1561	25.1100	-29.03	518.24
13-Jul-18	Bought	2.1183	12.1700	-25.78	492.46
13-Jul-18	Div			51.12	543.58

ensure the figures are correct.

- The last column, "Balance", is the amount which should match the broker's cash balance when you've made all entries.
- The cash balance of each account would appear on the Summary report, which is where you balance the shares and cash to the broker account.

You would then record the transaction (buying, dividends reinvested or selling) in an individual stock worksheet. The left side is to record New Purchases, the right side is for reinvested dividends. Sales would be negative entries.

The totals at the bottom would be linked to the Summary report (the amounts/figures will automatically show in the Summary).

Here is a sample of an individual stock transaction entry worksheet:

Sample Stock 1									
Settlement Date	Action	Number of Shares	Price Per Share	Comm Fee	Number of Share Bal	ACB (Investment)	ACB per Share	Capital Gain (Loss)	Dividend Shares
3-Mar	Buy	100	$50.00	$10	100	$5,010.00	$50.10	–	0.00
1-May	Sell	-50	$120.00	$10	50	$2,505.00	$50.10	3,485.00	0.00
18-Jul	Buy	50	$130.00	$10	100	$9,015.00	$90.15	0.00	0.00
25-Sep	Sell	-40	$90.00	$10	60	$5,409.00	$90.15	-16.00	0.00
26-Sep	Div	1	$98.00	$0	61	$5,507.00	$90.28	0.00	1.00
27-Sep	Div	1	$120.00	$0	62	$5,627.00	$90.76	0.00	1.00
					62	$5,627.00	$90.76	0.00	0.00
				Totals	62	$5,627.00	$90.76		2.00

Record your Buys, Sells and the Dividend Reinvestments, for each stock on a similar worksheet. I've separated the stocks by accounts, TFSA, RRSP/RRIF, Non-Registered and even DRIP accounts. I've allowed for 10 stocks in each category. You add additional one, but you'll have to add them to the Summary report, in the right section and adjust the formulas.

Here's part of a Summary Report (a sample):

					Portfolio Summary Report				
TFSA Stocks	Adj Cost Base	ADC Per Share	Dividend Shares	Bought Shares	Number of Shares	DIV	Yearly Div	Ave Yield	Qt
1st	$5,627.00	$90.76	$2.00	$60.00	62.0000	3.60	$223.20	3.97%	
2nd	#DIV/0!	#DIV/0!	0.0000	$0.00	0.0000	1.00	$0.00	#DIV/0!	
3rd	#DIV/0!	#DIV/0!	0.0000	$0.00	0.0000	1.00	$0.00	#DIV/0!	
4th	#DIV/0!	#DIV/0!	0.0000	$0.00	0.0000	1.00	$0.00	#DIV/0!	
5th	#DIV/0!	#DIV/0!	0.0000	$0.00	0.0000	1.00	$0.00	#DIV/0!	
6th	#DIV/0!	#DIV/0!	0.0000	$0.00	0.0000	1.00	$0.00	#DIV/0!	
7th	#DIV/0!	#DIV/0!	0.0000	$0.00	0.0000	1.00	$0.00	#DIV/0!	
8th	#DIV/0!	#DIV/0!	0.0000	$0.00	0.0000	1.00	$0.00	#DIV/0!	
9th	#DIV/0!	#DIV/0!	0.0000	$0.00	0.0000	1.00	$0.00	#DIV/0!	
10th	#DIV/0!	#DIV/0!	0.0000	$0.00	0.0000	1.00	$0.00	#DIV/0!	
Total TFSA	#DIV/0!		2.0000	60.0000	62.0000		$223.20	#DIV/0!	
Un-Invested	$0.00								

Look at the "1st" line and see that the figures match the Transaction totals above.
When the annual dividend paid by the "**Div**"

"Number of Shares" column MUST match with the number of shares in your broker account for each stock. If out, check your individual stock entries.

Notice the tabs at the bottom. The RRSP and TFSA are the other sub-worksheets which is where you actually record the transactions.

These two reports, Transaction and Summary, are the key reports in my Excel worksheets. You can design many other worksheets to provide specific information to track your own stocks or use them to provide the information that's important to you. I cannot express how handy I find Excel for tracking my investments. However, if you are not as familiar with Excel, I hope you can learn to use it, even if you only have a very elementary understanding of a basic worksheet. (Or, perhaps you could have a friend, or your kids or even your grandkids help you out). You may have your own method of recording, so my explanation is brief. Here is reminder that you can download samples of my Excel worksheets to help you get started:

You can Download my "Cdn Stock ACB Report Summary" Excel worksheet at:

https://drive.google.com/drive/u/1/folders/1kD-ZtK7WkIINobzB3HYJ1tnwnh9P3NDf

The sample worksheet includes:

- Summary Report
- TFSA: Stock Transaction worksheet - 10 stocks
- RRSP: Stock Transaction worksheet - 10 stocks
- Non-Reg: Stock Transaction worksheet- 10 stocks
- DRIP: Stock Transaction worksheet - 10 stocks
- Yield Projection

- Dividend Growth (DivGth) Calculation
- 10-Yr Average Yield (%Gth Yld) Calculation
- TSX 60 Listing & Exercise sheet
- NOBL Listing & Exercise sheet
- ACB Sample
- And others

NOTE:
1. The Adjusted Cost Base (ACB) for each stock will be calculated with each transaction.
2. The ACB per share is also show.
3. Capital Gains or Losses are shown when all or a portion of your stocks are sold.
4. Remember to update the annual dividend paid, when a company increases or cuts their dividend.
5. Save your worksheet every time you make entries.
6. Save the worksheet, under a different name at the end of each month, or for sure at the end of each year.

Again, whether you use my sample reports or your own, it is extremely important to **backup** your worksheets often. At year-end I always make a backup copy and name it: 2020_12 Stock Summary (for easy reference). When you make the next years' entries, it will change the totals and you will not be able to see certain data from the previous year-end. By having a backup each year, you will be able to go back to see how the previous year ended.

I promise that once you've used Excel for a while making the entries will become easy and fast. I probably spend less than 20 minutes a week making entries, but spend more time watching the changes each entry has on my total income. Some would say watching paint dry is faster, but I argue, it's definitely not as satisfying!

Forget the basic rules of investing:

I doubt there are many investors, advisors and investing books which do not recommend or at least consider Diversification, Asset Allocation and Rebalancing as basic and sound investing rules. Their main objective is to protect the investor's capital and limit investor's risk. Sound advice and who would disagree?

In the Foreword, Tom Connolly said, "As you are most likely just beginning with dividend growth, some of what you encounter may have to be taken on faith for a while. It is truly unbelievable."

I also mentioned at the beginning, "We're not going to play their game of needing to beat the market, rather, we'll play our own game, with our own rules, ignoring the market altogether". Going against the basics of Investing 101, diversification, asset allocation and rebalancing, is where I ask you to take me on faith or at least consider my reasoning. If you see the merit in what I've presented so far, I hope that as I continue, you'll see how, "breaking the rules" is actually how you "beat the game". That I differ from more traditional investing strategies is the key to achieving our objective: generating a growing income from our investments.

In this section, I will define these terms, and provide explanations why they don't necessarily work within my income investment strategy parameters.

Diversification:

Common definition: "Diversification is a technique that reduces risk by allocating investments among various financial instruments, industries, and other categories. It aims to maximize return by investing in different areas that would each react differently to the same event."

Rather than argue the point, I'll quote Warren Buffett:

> "Diversification is protection against ignorance. It makes little sense if you know what you are doing."

In other words, if you don't have the knowledge, time or know-how to identify quality investments, then covering all your bases might be a good way to go. However, you now have the four-rule test to quickly identify quality companies not just in Canada, but in the US and any other market. There is no need to dilute your holdings, lower your potential income or settle for below-average income returns.

Stick with large, stable and profitable companies with a long record of returning profits to its shareholders. I believe it relieves you of having to rely on diversification to mitigate market fluctuations. Diversify by selecting among the best stocks in every sector and in different markets. I'll repeat here that I prefer quality over quantity.

Another thing most forget is that during severe market corrections, recessions and crashes, ALL investments drop in value. The financial crisis of 2008 saw the market value of most portfolios drop by 35% or more. This included dividend growth portfolios. However, the difference was that dividend growth income investors did not see their income drop, though, to be fair, it grew at a slower rate. Fixed income was no protection, as interest rates dropped as well. There was a silver lining for the DG income investor, actually all investors, as the severe drop in prices was a great opportunity to buy more shares at depressed prices. DG investors would have benefitted the most as they are not worried when prices would rise, in fact they prefer them to stay down longer, enabling them to earn even more income!

For those thinking of diversifying into foreign stocks, or Emerging or International ETFs, I suggest you consider the many US companies with exposure to foreign markets, like McDonald's, Procter & Gamble and Coca-Cola. Like international stocks, they generate the bulk of their income outside the US. Buying shares of US multinationals can be an effective way for investors to get exposure to the global economy with quality DG companies. They are all listed in the NOBL ETF, but still they should be carefully assessed before purchasing.

Asset Allocation:

Common Definition: "Asset allocation is an investment strategy that aims to balance risk and reward by apportioning a portfolio's assets according to an individual's goals, risk tolerance and investment horizon. The three main asset classes - equities, fixed-income, and cash and equivalents - have different levels of risk and return, so each will behave differently over time."

As an income investor, bonds, preferred stocks and other fixed assets would not make up any part of your investment portfolio. Our objective is for a growing income, not a fixed one. Fixed assets may have a place as part of one's savings or funds, often set aside for emergency or other needs, but they are not effective in growing one's income, which is our priority.

I recommend you maintain a 100% equity income investment portfolio of the best dividend growth stocks which you will have chosen after careful evaluation.

Rebalancing:

Common Definition: "The primary goal of a rebalancing strategy is to minimize risk relative to a target asset allocation, rather than to maximize returns. A portfolio's asset allocation is the major determinant of a portfolio's risk-and-return characteristics. Yet, over time, asset classes produce different returns, so the portfolio's asset allocation changes. Therefore, to recapture the portfolio's original risk-and-return characteristics, the portfolio should be rebalanced."

As an income investor we make every attempt to reduce risk, in advance, by screening out stocks which do not meet our criteria. I feel very confident with my four-rule test, even providing for exceptions to those rules in order to find the best possible dividend growing stocks we can. The objective is to maximize income regardless of how the market reacts or other assets perform over time.

Bonds and fixed income assets, again, play no part in our income investment. I do recommend holding cash reserves and keeping savings separate from your investments. Once you've taken the time to research and build your income investment portfolio, the only time you should consider rebalancing is if you reevaluate a company's performance and find it fails to meet your expectations.

If your current roster of companies continues to provide the income growth you expect, and its future looks bright, there is no reason to divest yourself of any of your current shares.

We want to maximize our income and avoid giving up our best holdings. If you want to increase your holdings of a particular stock or sector, buy those on your next purchase.

I also don't feel it's important to maintain an even percentage between all stocks or sectors. I don't recommend you have all your holdings in a very small number of stocks or a single sector, but I do subscribe to the'motto everything in moderation. Again, it's the income that is important and if you've built up a sizable holding of one company because you were able to buy it at a value-price, all the better. Never sell a good stock that keeps paying and growing your income.

Don't be swayed by the plethora of investment advice touting diversification, asset allocation and rebalancing. Trust your instincts, as I have, and resist the urge to "muck around" with your portfolio. Let others buy and sell to their heart's desire, all in the hopes of keeping their portfolios evenly distributed. I don't object if they do, it's just that I have learned through experience what suits my income goals and what is best for my investment portfolio.

The three "S's" of income investing

Simple: Income investing is one of the simplest forms of investing. By using the four-rule test to screen stocks you eliminate the lower quality dividend growth stocks. Evaluating company's past performance and deciding which stocks to add to your "List of stocks to consider" becomes a simple process. Once you've compiled your own List of stocks to consider, deciding which stocks to buy and when will be determined by the income the stocks will provide.

Sure: Income growth investing is a sure way to generate a growing income regardless of how the market reacts. By sticking with companies that have grown their earnings for long periods and regularly paid out a portion to shareholders, makes those future payments almost a certainty. By reinvesting the dividends you receive, you will generate income even if you stop adding funds to your portfolio.

Safe: Yes, there are risks with investing, but large, stable dividend growth companies are possibly the safest stocks one can find. As the companies pay and grow the dividend your investment becomes safer the longer you hold the stocks. That's the double dip, you receive more income over time and the value of your holdings will also rise, because your stock price will rise.

Chapter 5

I don't earn enough to invest in stocks!

Saving entails sacrifice; maybe that's why it brings rewards. (Mauricio Chaves Mesén, 12 Laws of Great Entrepreneurs)

Would you turn down someone if they handed you $20? How about $50 every three months, or even better $500/quarter or more? For those who think they don't have any spare money to invest in stocks, I am here to tell you that it simply isn't true. If you have enough money to buy lunch a couple times a month, then you have enough to start investing in dividend growth stocks. No matter how much one earns (or how little), you can start on the path to an ever-growing income. Make the effort to start saving and I'll show you how to make money on every cent you invest.

Even with an initial investment of $50 per month you could start generating income within one quarter, and you will be surprised how quickly your income will grow. And if you make a continuous effort to save, your quarterly income will become $50, then $100 per quarter and even more as time progresses.

For the small investor there are three basic investment choices:

1. A low-cost mutual fund
2. A low-cost or no-fee ETF, and
3. A company Dividend Reinvestment Plan (DRIP).

The first and second options charge little or no fees to purchase shares, but you will pay an annual fee on your holdings, even if it's as little as 0.05% or 1.5%, which adds up over time. As for mutual funds and ETFs, they are viable investment options, but you will have already read about my hesitations in choosing them over dividend growth stocks.

With the third option, a Dividend Reinvestment Plan (DRIP) you will pay **no** fees and will have every cent you invest working to grow your income. I believe this is the most ideal way to go when you are just starting out investing for income growth.

Dividend Reinvestment Plan (DRIP):

A Dividend Reinvestment Plan may be a lofty sounding investment property, but it is truly a simple and very efficient method of growing income. The most straightforward way to describe its advantages is that you can receive an income by owning shares of companies that pay a dividend. You can then earn even more money by reinvesting your dividends to buy more shares, thus, receiving a larger dividend on the next payment date. Your income will grow even faster if the company increases the dividend they pay and, as the cycle repeats, your income grows exponentially.

A more technical description, DRIPs are programs which allow current shareholders to use cash dividends to buy more shares from the company (through a Transfer Agent), bypassing the broker and brokerage commissions. However, to add additional money to a DRIP, participating companies must offer Share Purchase Plans (SPP), and unfortunately, not all do. SPPs allow existing shareholders to purchase further shares at no cost or commissions.

Some investors feel that DRIP accounts are "clunky" or labour intensive to open, making them less attractive to start with. I would argue that the effort made to open your DRIP will pay off, so don't be turned off by the work that appears to be involved. I have provided three ways to obtain your first share(s) needed to start your DRIP:

1   If you have a friend or relative who owns any of the shares listed in Appendix B, you can ask them to sell you one or more shares. To do this they would contact their broker and obtain a Share Certificate (probably at a total cost of $75) for the number of shares being transferred and have it put in your name. With the Share Certificate physically in hand, you would contact the company Transfer Agent, (companies that deal with either Computershare or AST as their transfer agent). Then complete the DRIP application form and send it in with the physical share certificate to the Transfer Agent.

1. Secondly, you could open a Discount Broker account and purchase a few shares of the company stock you want. You might want to purchase more than one share to reduce the overall cost to setup the DRIP. Once the shares are bought, ask the broker to transfer the shares to the company Transfer Agent, again either Computershare or AST Canada. The preferred method would be by Direct Registration Service (DRS). The DRS method does not require you to buy a Share Certificate, the shares will be transferred electronically but you will still pay a $75 fee.

2. The third method and probably least expensive, is to buy one share at the DRIP Resource Center (a website where individuals are willing to help others by selling one company share to enable them to start a DRIP accounthttp://www.dripinvesting.org/). I have provided a detailed step-by-step explanation of obtaining your first

share from the DRIP Resource Centre, starting the DRIP and recording all DRIP transactions in **Appendix B**.

I hope these steps do not seem difficult to follow, some have criticized their usefulness of DRIPs due to the steps (and fees) that accompany their set up. But I argue that the effort is worth the work because:

1. The dividends you receive in your DRIP will purchase fractions of shares which enhance compounding the income growth.
2. There are no commissions or fees to invest small or large amounts to buy shares.

However, to be fair, I should also provide some of the disadvantages of DRIPs:

1. It takes a bit of time to set up a DRIP, and any additional DRIPs,
2. You cannot purchase shares at a specified price,
3. Some feel you are restricting diversification (but I argue that you are sticking with quality), and
4. Some find the recording of DRIP transactions a hassle. (16 entries a year does not seem like a hassle to me.)

Initially your DRIP income from your savings will seem small. Don't get discouraged. Watch how your income keeps growing each quarter and even more so when you add more money to your holdings. Whenever possible increase the amount you save and the income will jump up again next quarter. This is the backbone of my philosophy of the ever-growing income.

I have $1,000 and more to invest. Now what?

> If you find a stock you like, buy a few shares to Test the Water. Wait a while and see how the stock does and if you still like it buy a bit more. By investing regularly one would Average Up when prices were rising and Average Down when prices fell. In the long-term your Average cost should always be lower than the current price. (John Bart, founder of ShareOwners Investment Inc.)

....

> It's not which dividend growth stock you buy, but when you buy it. (Tom Connolly, *The Connolly Report*)

If you are ready to invest larger amounts, you will need to open a discount investment account with a broker to purchase shares. Many of the Canadian banks have Investment divisions (see Appendix F for a partial list). If you can invest $1,000, $2,000, $5,000 or more, the DRIP process will seem cumbersome and restricting by not being able to buy immediately or at the price you wish.

A $1,000 investment will cost about a $9.95 commission, or 1%, of the total investment with most discount brokers (9.95/1000 x 100). $2,000 will cost a 0.50% fee and $4,500 a 0.22% fee. I'd suggest you try to keep the commissions to less than the 0.50%, always remember that the more money you can invest the lower your commission.

Even if you have larger sums to invest don't be tempted to expand your selection of Canadian stocks. Stick to the quality DG stocks you created from the TSX 60 using the four rules. Invest in individual Dividend Growth stocks and avoid ETFs, Bonds, preferred stocks and mutual funds. I feel very strongly they dilute your position rather than enhance it.

Build your holdings up slowly and over time. The thing to remember is that we are not playing the "price" game, rather the "income" game. What you want is to buy your stocks at a reasonable price, one which gives you the best yield for a stock (refer back to "When does price matter"). Once you actually buy, forget the price. The market constantly shifts, as will the price of a stock and that is what we are trying to avoid, the anxiety of market-watching. It's not that price isn't important, as I explained earlier in the book, it just isn't our priority.

Refer back to "How, where and what to invest" when deciding which account to use to purchase your stocks. I believe you should max out your TFSA, then the RESP, if you have children, and finally an RRSP. My reasoning is that your account needs usually match your current income situation. As your income grows, you'll probably be able to max out all three accounts and then look at adding funds to a non-registered account.

Again, depending on how much you have to invest, spread your investment over one or two stocks, keeping your commission low.

I already have a portfolio of ETFs and growth stocks, why change?

If you are content with your portfolio's performance than why consider a change? Good question, but I believe there are several good reasons to consider switching to dividend

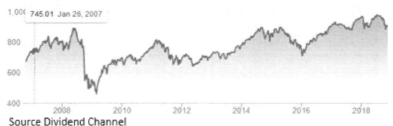

Source Dividend Channel

growth income investing:

1. If your portfolio consists mainly of ETFs and growth stocks, then your portfolio value is dependent upon the market and stock prices. Since the financial crisis, the market has generally been on an upswing. However, from its peak in June 2008, the market took until August 2014 (6 years) to recover from its 2009 low. That's how long it would have taken the value of your ETFs and growth stocks to recover.

2. It is worth asking yourself a number of questions: How much income is your current portfolio generating? How much has that income grown since 2008? If you consider some of the income growth examples we have provided, how does your income compare? Again, if you are dependent on market value, you now see the perils of traditional investing and hopefully, the advantages of income growth.

120

3. What do you think the value of your portfolio will be when the next major correction or crash occurs and how long might it take for your portfolio to recover? If you are like me, it is not a risk worth hanging my financial security on.

4. Would you expect the income from your portfolio to remain the same or even grow if there is a major correction? Even as I write this book, the market is extremely volatile, there is regular speculation on recession. This is stress you can avoid if you stop being dependent on price growth.

Est. Average GIC Rates		Inflation
2018	1.25%	2.20%
2017	1.00%	1.56%
2016	1.00%	1.50%
2015	1.00%	1.61%
2014	1.05%	1.47%
2013	1.05%	1.24%
2012	1.35%	0.83%
2011	1.30%	2.30%
2010	1.05%	2.35%
2009	1.20%	1.32%
2008	2.00%	1.16%
2007	2.70%	2.38%

5. Even with a healthy portion in fixed assets, look at average GIC interest rates and inflation from 2007 to 2018. Couple that with a 40% to 50% drop in stock prices and ask yourself how secure will your retirement income be when the next correction occurs? It is worth noting that drops in markets are

advantageous to growth income investing, as much as it is for other forms of investing.

I have not given specific reasons for you to consider changing strategies, as I don't have all the answers to the questions. What I do know is that we can predict with some certainty that there will be a major market correction in the future and likely the effect on one's portfolio will be similar to the effects of past corrections. However, if one focuses on income and an income growth method of investing, regardless of market fluctuations, your income should continue to grow, even if one's portfolio value decreases. This I know for a fact, I experienced this myself during the last major financial crisis. Both strategies can take advantage of low prices to buy more shares, but income investors will reap a double benefit when the market recovers, with price gain and lots of additional income.

You cannot control the value of your holdings, any more than you can control the market, but don't you think it would be nice to see consistent income growth, no matter how the market performs?

How do I switch to Income Investing?

If you do wish to switch to income investing, from ETFs and growth stocks, I suggest you "bite the bullet" on any ETFs or mutual funds you hold immediately. Sell them even if it means taking a loss. With the growth stocks you will want to select your own time to sell. If you already have a gain than sell right away, if not, you could hold to see if the market rises and sell at a break-even point or at a profit. If they have performed badly you might just need to sell and chalk the loss up to "experience".

Don't just buy any stock I have mentioned in this book or ones recommended by others without first developing your own List of Stocks to Consider. Take the time to go through the Four-rule test and select from the stocks on your own list. Again, don't worry about owning all the stocks, but try to buy those which are value-priced and offer a reasonable yield. Build your portfolio over time. Add new stocks in different sectors and seek the best not the most, remember quality over quantity.

I don't need the money. So why change my investments?

In investing, what is comfortable is rarely profitable.(Robert Arnott, portfolio manager, PIMCO All Asset)

There are seasoned investors, comfortable with their current investment strategy, probably with a 60/40 portfolio of investments, with GIC's, bonds and mutual funds. Content with the returns and satisfied with their current money flow, finding the energy needed to start an income growth investment fund may seem hard to muster.

I do have personal experience with such a person, someone who is retired, has a company pension, CPP and OAS, and was reluctant to change things up. They had cash savings of $35,000, mutual funds and GICs of $575,000 in a RRIF and TFSA, drawing down $5,000/year from GICs to cover expenses. Annual interest earned on investments was $16,000 or 2.8%.

However, because of the financial crisis in 2008, the mutual funds dropped in value and GIC rates were also low. This was enough for the person to ask for help to set up an income portfolio (we had discussed it several times in the past).

In 2015, here's what transpired:

- Opened an investment account at the bank with a RRIF, TFSA and Non-registered account.
- Sold the mutual funds and cashed in the GIC's without losing the interest.
- Invested in nine DG stocks. Three in a DRIP so the dividends would be deposited into a savings

account monthly (generating about $6,000 per year).

- As other GIC's matured, the money was invested in DG stocks.
- In 2017 sold a REIT and an agriculture stock which had cut their dividend. Funds reinvested.
- Reinvested all dividends.
- No other activity, such as selling, to rebalance.

Today, in 2018, there are eleven DG stocks in the RRIF, TFSA, Non-Registered and DRIP accounts. The DRIP now deposits $9,000 to the savings account, with no additional funds or stocks added, and the portfolio value (not market value) is now $650,000, generating $35,000 of dividend income or 5.38% (35,000/650,000 x100) per year. In three years, this person's annual investment income has doubled, and the income is no longer at the whim of the market. Not bad, I'd say!

They even began making the entries, recording the income and monitoring the increases. They still only need a very small amount of their investment to live on and are now planning on how to pass on their ever-growing income and investments to their beneficiaries. The person no longer worries about the market or price risks and expressed this opinion afterwards; "I wish I had done this years ago!"

Chapter 6

As an investor's time horizon lengthens equities become progressively less risky than bonds.(Warren Buffett, Letter, April 2018)

The proof is in the numbers:

The return on equities is equal to the current dividend yield plus dividend growth (plus or minus any valuation effect.(Buttonwood, *The Economist*)

Over the course of the book, I've made several statements and presented a system of investment that many might disagree with. One might have been wary of the contents of this book from the title, a lofty promise, an ever-growing income. After reading this far, I hope I have made the process of dividend growth investing clear, understandable, and most importantly, attainable.

But to be even more convinced, you might also be asking how much income can one earn from an income investment strategy?

It depends upon how much you are willing to invest and over what time frame. So, the answer is up to you, but look at the examples we've provided and the income growth rates. They have averaged a 10% compounded increase each year and with additional funds being added, you will accelerate the growth. So, it is very conceivable your income could grow to exceed your future annual expenses. I will always recommend that you save as much as you can, meeting your account maximums in as many cases as possible.

Let's go back to my grandson's figures presented in Chapter 1, where I showed how much income he earned each year. Maybe you were not that impressed with the original dividend income figures. I've re-calculated what his income would have been if the funds were deposited in a high interest rate saving account or in the XIU ETF.

The chart below shows the difference dividends, dividend increases and compounding can make.

Actual Div Income			Tangerine		XIU ETF		
Year	Div	% Gth	Div	% Gth	Div	% Gth
2008	$217.30		$191.00		$128.73	
2009	$253.81	16.80%	$95.17	-50.18%	$126.18	-1.98%
2010	$281.43	10.88%	$91.08	-4.29%	$135.35	7.27%
2011	$323.94	15.10%	$113.16	24.25%	$137.75	1.77%
2012	$379.31	17.09%	$106.44	-5.94%	$173.43	25.91%
2013	$431.32	13.71%	$105.14	-1.22%	$203.83	17.53%
2014	$481.32	11.59%	$106.49	1.29%	$225.77	10.76%
2015	$531.84	10.50%	$78.35	-26.42%	$249.90	10.69%
2016	$588.67	10.69%	$66.85	-14.68%	$189.72	-24.08%
2017	$655.52	11.36%	$73.72	10.28%	$267.25	40.87%
2018	$767.36	17.06%	$110.45	49.82%	$328.06	22.75%
Total	$4,911.82		$1,137.86		$2,165.95	
Tangerine	Diff	$3,773.96	331.67%			
XIU	Diff	$2,745.87	126.77%			

The interest paid by Tangerine was reinvested, as were the distributions from XIU over the 11 years. Look at the difference by investing in a quality DG stock makes, $3,773.96 more income and a whopping 331.67% difference over the saving account and $2,745.87 and 126.77% difference over XIU. That's income growth, compounding and what I call an ever-growing income!

Have you heard the phrase: "Show me the money" made famous by characters in the 1996 film *Jerry Maguire*? If you invest in fixed income or low-growth investment products (i.e. Bonds and ETFs), you'll be asking yourself, "Where is the money?" instead!

Let's look at an actual stock purchase example where larger amounts were invested over a short period, of 4 years:

	Invested	Income	Tot Invest	Inc % Gth
2011	$13,300	$181	$13,481	
2012	$24,680	$1,390	$39,551	667.96%
2013	$50,000	$3,739	$93,290	168.99%
2014	$41,000	$5,711	$140,001	52.74%
2015	$0	$9,295	$149,296	62.76%
2016	$0	$10,162	$159,458	9.33%
2017	$0	$11,179	$170,637	10.01%
2018	$0	$12,360	$182,997	10.56%
Totals	$128,980	$54,017	$182,997	
Ave Yld of Purchases	5.00%			
2018 Dividends	$12,360			
Yld on Total Investment	6.75%	(12,360/182,997)x100		

No other funds were added to the stock after 2014, other than reinvesting the dividends. 2016 to 2018 the three years where income growth is due to reinvesting the dividend and dividend increases. As with the other examples I have provided this stock is averaging 10% income growth each year. The other important figure is the Yield on Total Investment, which is showing at 6.75%. The average yield on all purchases was 5% (ranging from 4.3% to 5.5% over the 8 years), yet the overall yield and income is growing slowly and steadily and will likely continue year after year.

In Chapter 2 we said if one begins DG investing at age 60, they would need to invest larger amounts. This example might show the income they could generate over a short time and the type of yield on their investment they could obtain.

TFSA Results:

This next section provides a 10-year history of dividend investing that I am very familiar with, it belongs to my wife and me!

First, I want to summarize how you can achieve a growing income (these are practices I adhere to and have described throughout the book):

1. Save money for your retirement, separate from savings or emergency funds.
2. Invest regularly and if possible, increase the amount you save over time.
3. Invest your savings in quality dividend growth stocks selected by using the four-rule step process I have provided.
4. Avoid investing in fixed income bonds, GICs and preferred stocks, low-income growth mutual funds, ETFs or high yielding stocks.
5. Reinvest all dividends to enhance compounding.
6. Be conscious of the tax effects of investing in various accounts and products.
7. Do not sell your stocks unless one of your holdings cuts their dividend or no longer meets your income criteria.
8. Do not watch or worry about the price of your holdings or their market value.

My wife and I invested the maximum amounts into our TFSA accounts each January for a total of $57,500 each since 2009. I hold four DG stocks and my wife 5 in our TFSAs. All of our stocks are from the TSX 60, selected using the 4-rule test. Here's our 10-year summary:

Hm Tfsa	Orig Invest	Div (Inc)	% Gth	Orig + Div	Running Tot	Yield
2009	5,000.00	144.94		5,144.94	5,144.94	2.82%
2010	5,000.00	399.00	175.29%	5,399.00	10,543.94	3.78%
2011	5,000.00	862.35	116.13%	5,862.35	16,406.29	5.26%
2012	5,000.00	959.70	11.29%	5,959.70	22,365.99	4.29%
2013	5,500.00	1313.46	36.86%	6,813.46	29,179.45	4.50%
2014	5,500.00	1742.35	32.65%	7,242.35	36,421.80	4.78%
2015	10,000.00	2404.75	38.02%	12,404.75	48,826.55	4.93%
2016	5,500.00	3301.78	37.30%	8,801.78	57,628.33	5.73%
2017	5,500.00	3813.66	15.50%	9,313.66	66,941.99	5.70%
2018	5,500.00	4496.91	17.92%	9,996.91	76,938.90	5.84%
Totals	$57,500.00	$19,438.90			$76,938.90	

Rm Tfsa	Orig Invest	Div (Inc)	% Gth	Orig + Div	Running Tot	Yield
2009	5,000.00	129.82		5,129.82	5,129.82	2.53%
2010	5,000.00	399.00	207.35%	5,399.00	10,528.82	3.79%
2011	5,000.00	758.17	90.02%	5,758.17	16,286.99	4.66%
2012	5,000.00	1,116.20	47.22%	6,116.20	22,403.19	4.98%
2013	5,500.00	1,516.00	35.82%	7,016.00	29,419.19	5.15%
2014	5,500.00	2,182.03	43.93%	7,682.03	37,101.22	5.88%
2015	10,000.00	2,917.74	33.72%	12,917.74	50,018.96	5.83%
2016	5,500.00	3,661.32	25.48%	9,161.32	59,180.28	6.19%
2017	5,500.00	4,143.28	13.16%	9,643.28	68,823.56	6.02%
2018	5,500.00	4,750.65	14.66%	10,250.65	79,074.21	6.01%
Totals	$57,500.00	$21,574.21			$79,074.21	
		Our 2018			Total with Div	Yield on
	Original invest	Annual Div			Reinvest	Invest
2018 Combined	$115,000.00	$9,247.56			$156,013.11	5.93%

The chart shows the contributions made to each TFSA and summarizes the 10 years since it was started. Notice that the "Yield" column percentage, on the right (in each account) varies up and down each year, but gradually increases. There are several reasons for this:

1. The price of stock purchases varied.
2. The dividend increases varied.
3. We bought some higher yielding stocks, then sold them when they cut the dividend and eliminated some

that we felt would not provide the dividend growth we sought.

4. Stock prices may have fallen while the dividend increased.

The three columns I like to watch are:

- the gradual and continuous income growth each year,
- the "% Gth" (percentage growth) of the income year-over-year, and
- the "Yield" column, which is the yield on investment and is currently 5.93% for the combined yield of both TFSAs.

We've achieved these results with the "Steady Eddies" mentioned earlier. None are speculative or high yield stocks (even the ones we sold), we invested the maximum, didn't try to time the purchases, but with confidence, we just sat back and let the process do its work.

It is only fair to state here that there will always be new choices which appear to offer the same or better returns. New large companies, ETFs, mutual funds, REITs and British ADRs. You will even see new bond offerings which seem appealing, like CoPower's Green private Bonds, with a 5% yield, and a 6-year fixed-rate. These products are designed to attract investors with their enticing rates, but you need to recognize that the rate is fixed and will not grow, while the others will just dilute your holdings. They offer short-term sparkle, but no long-term value.

Never forget, though, it is not in dividend stocks or high-interest fixed-rates, but with dividend growth stocks you will achieve your goal.

I started this book in the middle of 2018 and made reference to Star Trek and my own solution to the Market Kobayashi Maru:

- An alternative to seeking market returns and eliminating the reliance on market returns.
- A system where your returns are not tied to price fluctuations and won't play a part in your investment decisions.

Little did I know that just as I finished, I would be looking at two financial headlines on December 31, 2018:

"Stock Markets Worldwide Close Out Worst Year Since 2008"

and

"The bad news is nobody made money in 2018; the good news, markets are expecting the worst....To add some further perspective, a whopping 89 per cent of assets handed investors losses in 2018, the most in 117 years."

The TSX Index (3,800 holdings) was down 11.64%, the TSX 60 was down 7.58% and our own portfolio value was down 7.33% for 2018.

However, throughout this book I have insisted that we ignore the market and its effect on holdings and, instead, I have shown you, with all the account examples, that they have increased their income each year (actually more than 10% for 2018 despite the worst market performance since 2008). Our own portfolio income (actual dividends received) was up 10.72% over 2017. I imagine some skeptical of this strategy would think *"nice work if you can get it"*, but you can! Generate your own ever-growing income through diligence, patience and discipline, following the process described. Who wouldn't want an alternative to worrying if the market will continue its downward trend, if it recovers or goes sideways?

Let others be concerned with market gyrations, income investors can ignore the market and smile as our income continues to grow.

It's the growing income from your dividend growth payers that should always remain your focus, as well as the growing yield. A growing yield indicates that you are earning more income with less money invested. In other words, "it costs you less to receive $1 dollar of income as time passes. Fixed income or low-growth products simply cannot provide you with the same steady income growth over time that comes from a growing yield.

This brings us to what has become my mantra, and conveniently the title of my book:

Your Ever Growing Income: The Rising Yield on investments

How much money do you need to save to retire?

A dividend growth retirement portfolio allows us to continue building wealth after retirement. (Tom Connolly, 2014)

I'm sure you've read many articles asking this very question. And I am sure you have heard the same suggestion, of at least a million dollars! This magical number is often used because most believe a million-dollar portfolio can generate approximately $40,000 of annual income (allowing for a basic 4% interest rate: $1Million x 0.40% = $40,000). Is this a realistic goal for the average investor? I'll argue as an income investor, that you'll need much less to generate $40,000 of annual income, if that amount seems a reasonable retirement goal. As I've mentioned several times in this book, the longer you hold quality dividend growth stocks, the greater the income and the higher the yield on your investments!

Earlier, I showed you how my TFSA has performed. My wife and I have invested a total of $156,013 as of 2018, and our income is $9,248, giving us a yield on our TFSA investment of 5.93%.

If the 5.93% yield remains the same over time, (if anything, I expect the yield to increase), we will earn $40,000 of income from our TFSA's alone when our total investment reaches $674,829. To calculate this, divide your expected income, I suggest the example of $40,000, by your current income $9,247 (40,000/9,247 = 4.3257), then multiply the result by your current total investment, $156,013 x 4.3257. This will result in a final investment total of $674,869.

$675,000.00 might seem high for TFSA savings alone, but most likely you will have other investments, such as an RRSP, which will likely become the larger portion of your portfolio. The point is that if you invest with DG stocks throughout your entire portfolio, your yield on your entire portfolio will grow steadily and continuously. So, if $40,000 is your income goal and, if you invest wholly in DG stocks, it will take much less than one-million dollars to achieve financial freedom!

IMPORTANT I mentioned that our portfolio income rose 10.72% over last year, but I'd like to point out that we received that money for doing nothing. The companies paid us dividends, which were automatically reinvested and all of the companies raised their dividend during 2018, but we did not contribute a cent. Here's the most important takeaway from my entire investing philosophy, ***if you invest in quality DG stocks to generate an income, the companies also contribute by paying you a dividend. You reinvest the dividends to buy more shares and increase your income. Finally, when the companies raise the dividend on all the shares you own it further grows your income. You continue to add funds and the process accelerates. In other words, they are helping you to grow your income by adding to what you contribute, so you don't need to save as much to reach your income goal!*** That's how and why the yield on your investment rises. Please read this paragraph a few times so that you fully grasp its meaning.

I cannot stress enough the concept of the **Rising Yield**, because it's the key to earning enough income to retire without having to depend on selling your capital or needing to invest larger sums to obtain the same results. Those who invest for capital appreciation (the price rising) need and hope the price goes up continuously, which it never does and is a risky endeavor. I'll again refer to our own portfolio which dropped in value by 7.33% in 2018. In order to get back to our 2017 value we need a 7.91% increase. The larger the drop the greater the increase needed to recover. Imagine a 50% drop requiring a 100% increase to get back to the original value. No one wants to be a slave to the temperamental market, nervously watching price Through the use of my investment strategies I have not had to worry about market performance for over a decade.

To me, it's such a simple concept that I wonder why so few recognize it. ***The longer you hold shares of solid dividend growth stocks, the greater your income and yield will become***.

That's the point I am trying to get across with my book, if you invest regularly, reinvest the dividends, continue to buy more shares (the lower the price the better) and receive regular dividend increases, then there is no reason not to expect to retire with a steadily growing income to meet future needs. When you track your progress, as I have shown throughout the book, you will know long before you retire just how well you're doing. And if you're like me, you will gain a lot of comfort knowing your future is on its way to being financially secure. You won't be wondering "how much do I need to save", instead you will see your income steadily increase, encouraging you to save even more and invest in more solid DG stocks.

My friend Mark Seed, of the blog, "*My Own Advisor*" (https://www.myownadvisor.ca/), is a dividend investor and has set a retirement financial goal of $30,000/year from his investments, primarily through his dividend growth stocks.

He updates his progress monthly and shows the progress yearly on a chart. He's well on his way and will likely achieve his goal sooner than projected. Mark is a great example of how successful this form of investing can be, with patience and dedication, even providing a path to early retirement!

I have not mentioned the large number of followers of Tom Connolly. They are the silent, contented, and extremely grateful group that we rarely hear from, who, like me, discovered dividend growth investing and are now reaping the benefits. After employing patience and persistence, they are just enjoying their retirement.

Although I am advocating a singular form of investing, one that seems counterintuitive to most popular forms of portfolio building, I am very confident that you can and will benefit from it in ways that other forms of investing cannot provide. Income investing does require patience, it's a long-haul form of income growth, but in the end, aren't we all looking for the same end goal? To have enough money to see us through retirement in financial security and comfort! I believe very strongly that if you set your own income goal and follow my lead, you will not worry about having to beat the market, or stress over annual returns. As your investment grows, so will your income at an increasing rate, especially if your yield is increasing. **Don't get sidetracked by trying to rush or speed things up by chasing yield.**

One last point: if you are a retired investor and regardless if your retirement dividends surpass your living expenses or not, you often hear recommendations to change your current investment strategy by increasing the fixed asset allocation.

Standard "advice" from financial advisors to retirees is to reduce your equity positions to bonds, or other fixed assets, ("you almost certainly want exposure to bonds in your portfolio, with your exact weighting tied to your age, risk tolerance, investing goals and such" Rob Carrick). So, if my wife and I were to follow such advice, we'd be 77% bonds or other fixed assets and most likely giving up the larger portion of our growing income each year (10.72% for 2018) for a fixed income? Thanks, but no thanks!

Instead, I suggest that you stick to your dividend growth stocks in retirement, as we do, sit back and continue collecting those ever-rising dividends and a higher income each year.

Oh, did I mention one of the biggest advantages of this strategy? You'll look forward with joyful anticipation to receiving your dividend payment, and the joy you feel only increases as your dividends increase!

I opened with a Star Trek analogy. I hope you'll indulge me as I close with one.

Our mission: to explore strange new sources of income, to seek out quality, dividend growth companies, to boldly go where no other investing book has gone before (and guide you to your own path of an ever-growing income!)

Final Comments:

I'd like to take the opportunity to provide a list of lessons I've learned and important points to remember if you're seriously interested in starting this journey with income growth investing:

- A stock has no real value unless it pays a dividend.
- If a company does not pay a dividend, avoid, otherwise you are completely dependent on the price rising and your only return is when/if you sell the stock.
- It's not just which dividend stock, but which **dividend growth** stock to buy. Be conscious of what to buy and when. When stock prices go down, your stock purchases rise, and you will generate more retirement income.
- Dividend growth is about future earnings, not current earnings.
- Always require dividend growth year after year, this will lead you to finding high quality stocks (ones which have rising earnings year after year).
- Diversification is not the answer, instead concentrate on holding only quality dividend growth stocks.
- In the long-term, dividend growth encourages the price of the stock to grow.
- Let dividend yield and yield on investment be your benchmark, not whether your portfolio beats the market index.

Definitions:

Bond:

A fixed income investment where one lends money for a fixed interest rate for a set period of time. You can also purchase a Bond ETF, comprised of many bonds bundled together.

Dividends:

A part of a company's profits which are distributed to shareholders. Dividends may be in the form of cash or shares. Cash payments are paid out on a per share basis, ex: $1.20 per share, or $0.30 paid quarterly.

Dividend Payout Ratio:

The portion of earnings paid out as dividends to shareholders, typically expressed as a percentage. The payout ratio can also be expressed as dividends paid out as a portion of cash flow.

DRIP:

Dividend Reinvestment Plan. The cash dividends paid by a company are used to buy more shares of the company without any fees.

DRS:

Direct Registration Service. A procedure to transfer shares, without a Share Certificate.

Earnings:	The earnings of a business are the same as its net income or its profit. Either term means the same thing. Earnings are usually calculated as all revenues (sales) minus the cost of sales, operating expenses, and taxes, over a given period of time (usually a quarter or a year).
Free Cash Flow	Free Cash Flow per share (FCF) is a measure of a company's financial flexibility and is determined by dividing free cash flow by the total number of shares outstanding.
Investment:	The action or process of investing money for profit.
P/E Ratio:	P/E is short for the ratio of a company's share price to its per-share earnings.
Portfolio	The total of your investments, which may include, cash, TFSA, RRSP or RRIF, Non-registered accounts, DRIP, physical Gold and other investments.
Share Certificate:	A written document that is signed on behalf of a corporation to serve as a legal proof of ownership of number of shares.

SPP:	Share Purchase Plan. One can invest additional funds to buy shares without having to pay a commission.
Stock (or Shares):	A share in the ownership of a company. Stock represents a claim on the company's assets and earnings.
Total Investment:	The total amount of financial resources that a person has in a project. Includes original investments, re-invested dividends and new funds added to a portfolio.
Yield	Is the annual dividend divided by the current share price of a stock.
Yield on Investment	Total portfolio dividends divided by the total investment (not market value) of your portfolio.

APPENDIX A

TSX 60 Stocks

	Symbol	Company	Sector
1	AEM	Agnico Eagle Mines Limited	Materials
2	ATD.B	Alimentation Couche-Tard Inc.	Consumer Staples
3	ARX	ARC Resources Ltd.	Energy
4	BMO	Bank of Montreal	Financials
5	BNS	Bank of Nova Scotia	Financials
6	ABX	Barrick Gold Corporation	Materials
7	BHC	Bausch Health Companies Inc.	Health Care
8	BCE	BCE Inc.	Telecommunication
9	BB	BlackBerry Limited	Information Tech
10	BBD.B	Bombardier Inc.	Industrials
11	BAM.A	Brookfield Asset Management Inc.	Financials
12	CCO	Cameco Corporation	Energy
13	CM	Canadian Imperial Bank of Commerce	Financials
14	CNR	Canadian National Railway Company	Industrials
15	CNQ	Canadian Natural Resources Limited	Energy
16	CP	Canadian Pacific Railway Limited	Industrials
17	CTC.A	Canadian Tire Corporation, Limited	Consumer Disc
18	CCL.B	CCL Industries Inc.	Materials
19	CVE	Cenovus Energy Inc.	Energy
20	GIB.A	CGI Group Inc.	Information Tech
21	CSU	Constellation Software Inc.	Information Tech
22	CPG	Crescent Point Energy Corp.	Energy
23	DOL	Dollarama Inc.	Consumer Disc
24	EMA	Emera Incorporated	Utilities

25	ENB	Enbridge Inc.	Energy
26	ECA	Encana Corporation	Energy
27	FM	First Quantum Minerals Ltd.	Materials
28	FTS	Fortis Inc.	Utilities
29	FNV	Franco-Nevada Corporation	Materials
30	WN	George Weston Limited	Consumer Staples
31	GIL	Gildan Activewear Inc.	Consumer Disc
32	G	Goldcorp Inc.	Materials
33	HSE	Husky Energy Inc.	Energy
34	IMO	Imperial Oil Limited	Energy
35	IPL	Inter Pipeline Ltd.	Energy
36	K	Kinross Gold Corporation	Materials
37	L	Loblaw Companies Limited	Consumer Staples
38	MG	Magna International Inc.	Consumer Disc
39	MFC	Manulife Financial Corporation	Financials
40	MRU	Metro Inc.	Consumer Staples
41	NA	National Bank of Canada	Financials
42	NTR	Nutrien Inc.	Materials
43	OTEX	Open Text Corporation	Information Tech
44	PPL	Pembina Pipeline Corporation	Energy
45	POW	Power Corporation of Canada	Financials
46	QSR	Restaurant Brands International Inc	Consumer Disc
47	RCI.B	Rogers Communications Inc.	Telecom
48	RY	Royal Bank of Canada	Financials
49	SAP	Saputo Inc.	Consumer Staples
50	SJR.B	Shaw Communications Inc.	Telecom
51	SNC	SNC-Lavalin Group Inc.	Industrials
52	SLF	Sun Life Financial Inc.	Financials
53	SU	Suncor Energy Inc.	Energy

54	TECK.B	Teck Resources Limited	Materials
55	T	Telus Corporation	Telecom
56	TRI	Thomson Reuters Corporation	Consumer Disc
57	TD	Toronto-Dominion Bank	Financials
58	TRP	TransCanada Corporation	Energy
59	WCN	Waste Connections US Inc.	Industrials
60	WPM	Wheaton Precious Metals Corp	Materials

APPENDIX B

Finding company stocks offering DRIPs and SPP:

As of this writing, there are 30 Canadian stocks which offer

1	NAME	TICKER	DRIP	SPP	DISC	FEES	SPP MIN
2	Agnico Eagle Mines	AEM	Y	Y	5%	N	$500
3	*Alamos Gold*	*AGI*	*Y*	*Y*	*5%*	*N*	*$500*
4	AltaGas	ALA	Y	Y	3%	N	1000
5	Bank of Montreal	BMO	Y	Y	N	N	$0
6	Bank of Nova Scotia	BNS	Y	Y	N	N	$100
7	BCE	BCE	Y	Y	N	N	0
8	CAE	CAE	Y	Y	2%	N	$1,000
9	CIBC	CM	Y	Y	2%	N	$100
10	Emera	EMA	Y	Y	5%	N	$25
11	Enbridge	ENB	Y	Y	2%	N	0
12	*Enbridge Inc Fund*	*ENF*	*Y*	*Y*	*2%*	*N*	*0*
13	Exchange Income Crp	EIF	Y	Y	3%	N	$100
14	Firm Capital Corp	FC	Y	Y	3%	N	$250
15	First Quantum Minerals	FM	Y	Y	3%	N	$100
16	Fortis	FTS	Y	Y	2%	N	$100
17	IA Financial Group	IAG	Y	Y	N	N	$100
18	Imperial Oil	IMO	Y	Y	N	N	$50
19	Laurentian Bank	LB	Y	Y	2%	N	$500
20	Manulife	MFC	Y	Y	N	N	$100
21	National Bank	NA	Y	Y	N	N	$500
22	Olympia Fin. Trust	OLY	Y	Y	N	N	$1,000

DRIP and SPP.

23	Pengrowth Energy	PGF	Y	Y	5%	N	0
24	Sun Life	SLF	Y	Y	N	N	$100
25	Suncor	SU	Y	Y	N	N	$100
26	Superior Plus	SPB	Y	Y	4%	N	$1,000
27	Telus	T	Y	Y	N	N	$100
28	Temple Hotels	TPH	Y	Y	4%	N	$1,000
29	TransAlta	TA	Y	Y	3%	N	$0
30	TransCanada	TRP	Y	Y	2%	N	$50

If you apply my four-rule criteria for stock picking, you might end up with a dozen or so companies. You may yet eliminate any stocks with minimum SPP of more than $100, like I did, finally ending up with a total of 9 stocks (I excluded ENB as they suspended their DRIP plan in November 2018). The company stated that "...(ENB) has elected to suspend the DRIP at this time given substantial progress on its funding and asset sales plan, which will allow it to meet any remaining equity requirement for the balance of its currently secured growth program."

1	NAME	SBM	DRIP	SPP	DISC	SPP MIN
2	Bank of Montreal	BMO	Y	Y	N	$0
3	Bank of Nova Scotia	BNS	Y	Y	N	$100
4	BCE	BCE	Y	Y	N	0
5	CIBC	CM	Y	Y	2%	$100
6	Emera	EMA	Y	Y	5%	$25
7	Enbridge	ENB	Y	Y	2%	0
8	Fortis	FTS	Y	Y	2%	$100
9	Sun Life	SLF	Y	Y	N	$100
10	Telus	T	Y	Y	N	$100
11	TransCanada	TRP	Y	Y	2%	$50

After applying the four-rule test, I have chosen nine companies in four sectors, all listed in the TSX 60, and provided below:

Three Banks:
> **BMO – paid a dividend since 1820's**
> **BNS – paid a dividend since 1932**
> **CIBC – paid a dividend since 1868**

Two Utility Companies
> **Emera – Utility Company**
> **Fortis – Long history of raising its dividend**

Two Communication Companies
> **BCE – largest Communication Company in Canada**
> **Telus – A company with one with the best dividend history**

One Pipelines
> **TransCanada Corp – Held dividend through financial crisis**

One Insurance Company
> **Sun Life Financial – Affected by low interest rates, but held its dividend payments**

With only nine stocks to choose from it should not be too difficult to decide which would be a suitable choice to begin your DRIP portfolio.

I have described three ways to get your first share or shares to start your DRIP. At this time, I would like to expand on the third method I provided, which is to buy one share at the DRIP Resource Center:
http://www.dripinvesting.org/Boards/BoardMsgs.asp?BID=8

- Being a new user click on "Post New"
- You will then be asked to go to the Logon/Registration
- Complete the registration form

- Once completed you will be able to sign in, view new posts, respond to posts and add your own post where you can list a stock or stocks you are interested in acquiring.
- If you find a post listing a stock that you interested in, respond by providing your email.
- If the person still has the stock available, they will inform you of the cost of a share, usually the current market price, plus a handling fee of $10 or $15.
- If you accept, mail a cheque and be sure to provide the exact name, or names, the stock is to be listed under. If you are buying a stock for a minor, you must provide an adult name and the full name of the child.
- You will receive the Share Certificate in the mail in approximately two weeks.

Starting a DRIP

- You will contact the Transfer Agent (Computershare or AST) to obtain and complete the DRIP application form.
- When you have the Share Certificate send it to the Transfer Agent with the application form. You may wish to send a cheque to buy more shares at the same time.
- Once the DRIP is established the Transfer Agent will send you a new Share Certificate and you will begin receiving dividends.
- You can also go to their website and register to access your account information online.
- Now the easy part, anytime you want to add money, send a cheque or use the Direct Debit option, for those companies which accept them, to buy more shares.

- Try to add more money monthly, but don't worry if you are not able to add funds each month. Your income will continue to grow all on its own.
- Increase the amount you add to the DRIP, as your earnings increase.
- The Transfer Agent will use the dividend you receive and any extra funds you send in, to buy more shares, even if it's only a fraction of a share!
- Every quarter the Transfer Agent will send you a statement. If you go paperless, you can access their website to see how many new shares you've received and the total number of shares you own.
- Ignore the price of your company stocks, just enjoy watching your income growing each quarter.
- Record your DRIP transactions in your Excel spreadsheet, which I'll expand on in the next section.
- I encourage you, when you have the money, to start a second DRIP company stock, following the same process described earlier. However, if you find you have $1,000 or more to invest and can do so on a regular basis, open a TFSA with a broker and begin purchasing stocks directly. If you wish to obtain Full Dividend Reinvestment, ShareOwners Investment Inc. is the only broker providing such service?

How to record DRIP transactions:

Refer back to the end of Chapter 4. "Recording your investments". The recording of DRIP transactions is the same as with other portfolio accounts.

Final Comments on DRIPs

- When you buy shares from a broker to start a DRIP, besides the commission to buy the shares, you will be charged at least $75 for the DRS transfer for obtaining the Share Certificate.
- It's extremely important that when purchasing a Share Certificate, the name or names on the account are accurate.
- If you are starting a DRIP for yourself, and wish to share it with a spouse, you may want to include his/her name on the account. This will allow both to access the account information, especially useful if you need to speak directly with an agent by telephone.
- You can send money to the Transfer Agent anytime, but shares are bought at specific dates, depending on the company. They usually send you a list of the purchase dates for the company shares you own.
- The Transfer Agent Computershare accepts Direct Bank Debit for some companies. Direct Deposit is not available with AST companies. A cheque must be sent to AST with the order form to buy more shares.
- Some company stocks offer a discount on shares purchased, but that may change at any time.
- There are no fees or commissions charged by the Transfer Agent for managing the DRIP, buying shares with your dividends or to buy additional shares.
- At the end of the year, you will receive a T3 for tax purposes.
- If your total year-end taxable income is less than $40,000 you likely will not pay any tax on the dividends received.
- At some point there may be a tax advantage to opening a Tax-Free Savings Account (TFSA) with a discount broker. Your broker will handle the

transfer of the DRIP shares, by Direct Registration Service, to the TFSA account. Do not transfer more than the TFSA limit, currently $6,000/year or the maximum allowed. There is no cost to make the DRS transfer.

- Only a full number of shares can be transferred from one company to the next.
- Be sure to leave at least one full share in the DRIP account to keep it active.
- Continue investing funds into the DRIP and when the dividends or number of shares warrant, transfer more shares to the TFSA, leaving at least one share in the account.

Appendix C

57 Dividend Aristocrat Stocks:

	Symbol	Company	Yield 2019	Payout Ratio
1	ABBV	AbbVie Inc.	5.40	54.27
2	ABT	Abbott Laboratories	1.80	44.57
3	ADM	Archer-Daniels-Midland	3.00	38.75
4	ADP	Automatic Data Proc.	2.30	73.08
5	AFL	AFLAC Incorporated	2.20	26.28
6	AOS	A.O. Smith Corporation	1.80	33.65
7	APD	Air Products and Chem	2.80	61.86
8	BDX	Becton Dickinson and Co	1.30	28.22
9	BEN	Franklin Resources Inc.	3.60	32.95
10	BF.B	Brown Forman Inc Class B	0.00	0.00
11	CAH	Cardinal Health Inc.	3.90	40.62
12	CAT	Caterpillar Inc.	2.60	30.88
13	CB	Chubb Limited	2.20	27.40
14	CINF	Cincinnati Financial Corp	2.60	64.43
15	CL	Colgate-Palmolive Co	2.60	56.38
16	CLX	Clorox Company (The)	2.60	67.25
17	CTAS	Cintas Corporation	1.10	34.57
18	CVX	Chevron Corporation	4.00	69.75
19	DOV	Dover Corporation	2.20	36.64
20	ECL	Ecolab Inc.	1.20	36.02
21	ED	Consolidated Edison Inc.	3.90	68.42
22	EMR	Emerson Electric Co	3.00	62.98
23	FRT	Federal Realty Inv Trust	3.10	66.76

	Symbol	Company	Yield 2019	Payout Ratio
24	GD	General Dynamics Corp	2.20	34.41
25	GPC	Genuine Parts Company	2.90	52.70
26	GWW	W.W. Grainger Inc.	1.80	32.35
27	HRL	Hormel Foods Corp	2.00	47.16
28	ITW	Illinois Tool Works Inc.	2.90	53.36
29	JNJ	Johnson & Johnson	2.70	44.21
30	KMB	Kimberly-Clark Corp	3.80	63.08
31	KO	Coca-Cola Company	3.30	76.07
32	LEG	Leggett &Platt Inc.	3.70	61.88
33	LIN	Linde plc	2.00	
34	LOW	Lowe's Companies Inc.	2.00	44.35
35	MCD	McDonald's Corp	2.60	60.30
36	MDT	Medtronic plc.	2.30	42.30
37	MKC	McCormick & Co	1.90	46.18
38	MMM	3M Company	2.70	54.45
39	NUE	Nucor Corporation	2.70	21.02
40	PBCT	People's United Financial	4.20	52.25
41	PEP	PepsiCo Inc.	3.30	67.91
42	PG	Procter & Gamble Co	3.00	68.19
43	PNR	Pentair plc.	1.70	26.21
44	PPG	PPG Industries Inc.	1.80	32.55
45	ROP	Roper Technologies Inc.	0.60	16.41
46	SHW	Sherwin-Williams Co	0.80	19.70
47	SPGI	S&P Global Inc.	1.10	24.52
48	SWK	Stanley Black & Decker	2.10	32.36
49	SYY	Sysco Corporation	2.50	51.71

	Symbol	Company	Yield 2019	Payout Ratio
50	T	AT&T Inc.	6.90	59.44
51	TGT	Target Corporation	3.50	54.53
52	TROW	T. Rowe Price Group Inc.	3.10	40.44
53	UTX	United Technologies Corp	2.50	38.39
54	VFC	V.F. Corporation	2.40	
55	WBA	Walgreens Boots Alliance	2.50	29.44
56	WMT	Walmart Inc.	2.20	47.28
57	XOM	Exxon Mobil Corporation	4.50	43.95

Appendix D

Excel Worksheet Formulas

Tip: Not handy with Excel? Use Google!

	A	B	C	D	E	F	G	H	I	J	K
1	CNR										
2	2008	2009	2010	2011	2012	2013	2014	2015	2016	2017	Ave Yld
3	2.05%	1.76%	1.63%	1.62%	1.66%	1.42%	1.25%	1.62%	1.66%	1.59%	1.63%
5											Ave Yld
6											=AVERAGE(A3:J3)

1. Formula to calculate Average Dividend Yield:
2. Calculate div % growth each year (i.e. 10.87%, 5.88%, 20.37%) and% Gth over the years (in this case from 2008 to 2017 is 258.70%).

	A	B	C	D	E	F	G	H	I	J	K
1	CNR										
2	2008	2009	2010	2011	2012	2013	2014	2015	2016	2017	Ave Yld
3	0.46	0.51	0.54	0.65	0.75	0.86	1.00	1.25	1.50	1.65	258.70%
4		10.87%	5.88%	20.37%	15.38%	14.67%	16.28%	25.00%	20.00%	10.00%	

CNR										
2008	2009	2010	2011	2012	2013	2014	2015	2016	2017	Ave Yld
0.46	0.51	0.54	0.65	0.75	0.86	1	1.25	1.5	1.65	=(J3-A3)/A3
	=(B3-A3)/A3	=(C3-B3)/B3	=(D3-C3)/C3	=(E3-D3)/D3	=(F3-E3)/E3	=(G3-F3)/F3	=(H3-G3)/G3	=(I3-H3)/H3	=(J3-I3)/I3	

3. Yield projection, if price drops

Co.	Price Oct 15\18	Current Div	Current Yield	Ave 10 yr Yield	3% Price Drop	Yield	5% Price Drop	Yield	8% Price Drop	Yield	10% Price Drop	Yield
BCE	$51.56	$3.02	5.86%	4.89%	$50.01	6.04%	$48.98	6.17%	$47.44	6.37%	$46.40	6.51%
ENB	$40.96	$2.68	6.55%	3.33%	$39.73	7.60%	$38.91	7.76%	$37.68	8.01%	$36.86	8.19%

	Price Oct		Current	Ave 10 yr	3% Price		5% Price		8% Price		10% Price	
Co.	15\18	Current Div	Yield	Yield	Drop	Yield	Drop	Yield	Drop	Yield	Drop	Yield
BCE	51.56	=0.755*4	=C2/B2	0.0489	=B2*0.97	=$C$2/F2	=B2*0.95	=$C$2/H2	=B2*0.92	=$C$2/J2	=B2*0.9	=$C$2/L2
ENB	40.96	=0.671*4	=C3/B3	0.03325	=B3*0.97	=$C$2/F3	=B3*0.95	=$C$2/H3	=B3*0.92	=$C$2/J3	=B3*0.9	=$C$2/L3

		Total Invest	Org Shs	Div Shs	Total Shs	Av Cost	DIV	Yearly Div	Ave Yield	Qtr Div	Qtr $ Div
2	BNS	$18,457.46	246.7181	77.9625	324.6806	$56.85	3.40	$1,103.91	5.98%	0.85	$275.98
3	NA	$2,000.00	27.6052	0.0000	27.6052	$72.45	3.48	$96.07	4.80%	0.87	$24.02
4	SLF	$515.72	21.6920	0.5697	22.2617	$23.17	1.44	$32.06	6.22%	0.36	$8.01
	Total Investmen	$21,985.39	317.5485	78.7906	396.3391			$1,282.81	5.83%		
	Cash Balance	$543.58									

RRSP Stocks	Total Invest	Org Shs	Div Shs	Total Shs	Av Cost	DIV	Yearly Div	Ave Yield	Qtr Div	Qtr $ Div
1 FTS	$509.36	15.0240	0.2890	15.3130	$33.26	1.24	$18.99	3.73%	0.31	$4.75
2 NA	$512.17	7.2886	0.1596	7.4482	$68.76	3.48	$25.92	5.06%	0.87	$6.48
Total Investmen	$1,021.52	22.3127	0.4486	22.7613			$44.91	4.40%		
6 Grand Totals	$23,006.91	339.8611	79.2392	419.1003			$1,327.72	5.77%	Yield on Investment	

TFSA Stocks	Total Invest	Org Shs	Div Shs	Total Shs	Av Cost	DIV	Yearly Div	Ave Yield	Qtr Div	Qtr $ Div
BCE	='TFSA Stks'!AF165	='TFSA Stks'!AE163	='TFSA Stks'!AI163	=D3+E3	=C3/F3	2.33	=F3*H3	=I3/C3	=H3/4	=F3*K3
BNS	='TFSA Stks'!E218	='TFSA Stks'!C216	='TFSA Stks'!I216	=D4+E4	=C4/F4	3.4	=F4*H4	=I4/C4	=H4/4	=F4*K4
NA	='TFSA Stks'!AV165	='TFSA Stks'!AU163	='TFSA Stks'!AY163	=D5+E5	=C5/F5	3.48	=F5*H5	=I5/C5	=H5/4	=F5*K5
SLF	='TFSA Stks'!BD165	='TFSA Stks'!BC163	='TFSA Stks'!BG163	=D6+E6	=C6/F6	1.44	=F6*H6	=I6/C6	=H6/4	=F6*K6
Total Investr =SUM(C3:C6)	=SUM(D3:D6)	=SUM(E3:E6)	=SUM(F3:F6)			=SUM(I3:I6)	=I7/C7			
Cash Balanc =Activity!F8										

RRSP Stocks	Total Invest	Org Shs	Div Shs	Total Shs	Av Cost	DIV	Yearly Div	Ave Yield	Qtr Div	Qtr $ Div
FTS	='RRSP Stks'!D165	='RRSP Stks'!C163	='RRSP Stks'!G163	=D10+E10	=C10/F10	1.24	=F10*H10	=I10/C10	=H10/4	=F10*K10
NA	='RRSP Stks'!L165	='RRSP Stks'!K163	='RRSP Stks'!O163	=D11+E11	=C11/F11	=H5	=F11*H11	=I11/C11	=H11/4	=F11*K11
Total Investr =SUM(C10:C11)	=SUM(D10:D11)	=SUM(E10:E11)	=SUM(F10:F11)			=SUM(I10:I11)	=I12/C12			
Grand Totals =C12+C7	=D12+D7	=E12+E7	=F12+F7			=I12+I7	=I14/C14	Yield or		

How transaction total is "linked" to Summary report.

APPENDIX E

Six well established Canadian ETFs:

You can run the four-rule tests on these six ETFs or just look at their distribution charts on the right side and DivGth%. Would they qualify as good **income growth** investments, or even **capital growth** investments?

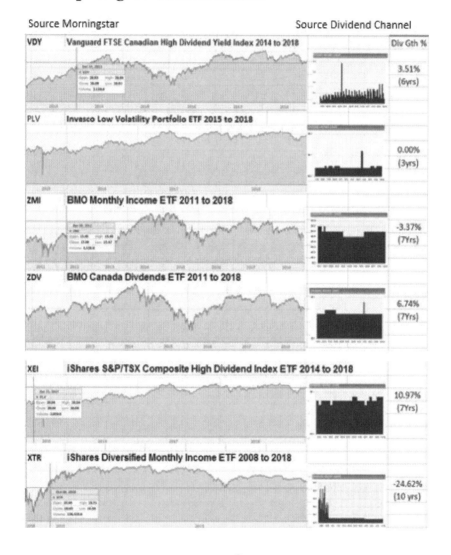

APPENDIX F:

Partial List of Canadian Discount Brokers

(Prices and amounts listed may not be current)

BMO InvestorLine	Discount	$9.95
CIBC Investors Edge	Discount	$6.95
Credential Direct	Discount	$8.88
HSBC InvestDirect	Discount	$9.88
Interactive Brokers	Discount	$1+
Presidents Choice	Discount	0.65%-1.40%
Questrade	Discount	$4.95+
QTrade	Discount	$8.75
RBC Direct Investing	Discount	$9.95
ShareOwners	Discount	$9.95-$20
Scotia i-Trade	Discount	$4.99-$25
Tangerine	Discount	1.07%
TD Direct Investing	Discount	$9.99
Trade Freedom	Discount	$9.95
TradeStation	Discount	$1+
Virtual Brokers	Discount	$9.99
WealthSimple	Robo advisor	0.0%-0.5%

APPENDIX G

Web sites recommended:

The Connolly Report – www.dividendgrowth.ca

Morningstar home page:
https://www.morningstar.ca/ca/membership/FeatureMatrix.as
px#334-hidenews

The Dividend Channel:
https://www.dividendchannel.com/history/?symbol=xiu.ca

Yahoo Finance:
https://ca.finance.yahoo.com/quote/ENB.TO/history?ltr=1

Dividend Growth Investing &
Retirement:https://www.dividendgrowthinvestingandretire
ment.com/canadian-dividend-all-star-list/

Canadian Shareowner Investments Inc.
http://www.investments.shareowner.com/home/v1/index.ht
ml

Computershare - https://www-
us.computershare.com/investor/?logout=ok&cc=CA&Server
Region=&lang=en&bhjs=1&fla=1&setting=cpu

AST Stock Transfer -
https://ca.astfinancial.com/answerline/getCifAccounts.do?l
ocale=en_CA

My Own Advisor
https://www.myownadvisor.ca/
https://www.myownadvisor.ca/helpful-sites/ (his helpful sites).

The DRIP Investing Resource Center - http://dripinvesting.org/Boards/BoardMsgs.asp?BID=8&N=2498

TSX Trading View - https://www.tradingview.com/symbols/TSX-BCE/

Drip Primer - http://www.dripprimer.ca/aboutdrips

Recommended books:

The Investment Zoo, by Stephen A. Jarislowsky. Published by Transcontinental, 2009

The Single Best Investment: Creating Wealth with Dividend Growth by Lowell Miller. Published by Print Project 2006

The Ultimate Dividend Playbook: Income, Insight and Independence for Today's Investor by Josh Peters. Published by Wiley 2007

The Dividend Rich Investor: Building Wealth with High Quality, Dividend-Paying Stocks by Joseph Tigue & Joseph Lisanti. Published by McGraw-Hill 1998

Double Your Money in America's Finest Companies by Bill Staton. Published by Wiley 2008

The Dividend Growth Investment Strategy by Roxann Klugman. Published by Kensington Publishing Corp. 2001

Beating the S&P with Dividends, by Peter O'Shea and Jonathan Worrall. Published by John Wiley & Sons 2005

The Strategic Dividend Investor, by Daniel Peris. Published by McGraw-Hill 2011

How not to move back in with your parents: the young person's complete guide to financial empowerment, by Rob Carrick. Published by Doubleday Canada 2012

My Other Books:

This is the US edition, which concentrates on US stocks for those who want to follow the Income Growth Investment Strategy in the American market.

The TFSA Compounder, shows you the advantages of investing in a TFSA first, before any other financial investments. It details how one can obtain financial freedom by combining your TFSA with the Income Growth Investment Strategy.

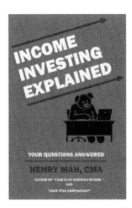

Income Investing Explained, addresses the investment decisions one needs to make after they have created their "List of Stocks to Consider". Which stocks to buy, when to buy, when to consider selling and how market conditions might change those decisions?

About the author

My wife Raelene and I are retired and we are both in our late 70s. I consider myself an average investor. I've made a lot of novice mistakes over the years and learned from them as well. I do not consider myself an investing guru. That distinction would best describe Tom Connolly, who has published *The Connolly Report* for 37 years, since 1981. I have been a loyal follower and consider Tom a friend and mentor.

I have achieved what I consider financial freedom by following the Income Investment strategy. Our success may not be exactly what you wish to achieve, as everyone has different goals and requirements, but I hope I can provide some inspiration to seriously contemplate adopting this investment strategy.

Another thing I'd like to add, we do not have a company pension. We live off our CPP, a clawed-back OAS and our dividend income. Currently our dividends exceed our living expenses, so we are able to reinvest approximately 60% of our profits to continue to grow our retirement income stream.

I hope that you have enjoyed learning about my investment strategy, and I would appreciate any comments or feedback, feel free to provide them on Amazon. I wish you all the best with your own investment journey. If you would like to contact me directly email me at:

HMyourgrowingincome@gmail.com

Join me on my blog:
https://risingyieldoninvestments.blogspot.com/